Nelson

Nelson

The Life and Letters of a Hero

ROGER MORRISS

COLLINS & BROWN

PUBLISHED IN ASSOCIATION WITH THE NATIONAL MARITIME MUSEUM

First published in Great Britain in 1996
by Collins & Brown Limited
London House
Great Eastern Wharf
Parkgate Road
London SW11 4NQ

Published in association with the National Maritime Museum

British Library Cataloguing-in-Publication Data:
A catalogue record for this book is available from the British Library.

ISBN 1 85585 274 8 (hb)
ISBN 1 85585 299 3 (pb)

1 3 5 7 9 8 6 4 2

Conceived, designed and edited by Collins & Brown Limited

Editors: Elizabeth Drury and Katie Bent
Picture Research: Philippa Lewis
Art Director: Roger Bristow
Designer: Bill Mason
Cover Design: Kevin Williams

Reproduction by Master Image, Singapore

Printed and bound in Hong Kong

FRONT COVER: *Portrait of Nelson by Lemuel Abbott, 1798-9. Composite painting of Nelson's principal ships, left to right the* Agamemnon, Vanguard, Elephant, Captain *and* Victory, *by Nicholas Pocock, 1807.*

BACK COVER: *Nelson's last letter to Emma Hamilton and her addendum, taken from* Some Stirring Relics of English History, *published by O. Anacker Ltd, 1936.*

FRONTISPIECE: *The fleet under Rear-Admiral Nelson at anchor in the Bay of Naples by Giacomo Guardi, 1798.*

C O N T E N T S

INTRODUCTION

NELSON IS BRITAIN'S GREATEST naval hero. His determination, daring and humanity had become a legend even before his overwhelming victory and his death at the Battle of Trafalgar in 1805. Every age since has found something to inspire it in his name, his ideas and his example.

At sea, Nelson combined experience and insight with a capability for precipitate action. Collingwood, his second-in-command at Trafalgar, observed some years before that battle how:

> Without much previous preparation or plan, he has the faculty of discovering advantages as they arise, and the good judgement to turn them to use. An enemy that commits a false step in his view is ruined, and it comes on him with an impetuosity that allows him no time to recover.

Such predatory power made Nelson a natural and invariably successful leader. Wellington, who encountered him by chance early in September 1805, in an ante-room of the Colonial Office, was struck initially by his absurd and charlatan manner: he talked in 'a style so vain and so silly as to surprise and almost disgust me.' But, by the time they parted, he was deeply impressed by Nelson's knowledge and ability to discuss international affairs with the wisdom and astuteness of a true statesman.

Yet there was something more about him besides military ability and wisdom in the 'heroic cast' that was observed in his lifetime. He consciously embodied heroism. From an early age he wanted to be a hero, and throughout his career he deliberately placed himself in challenging situations from which

RIGHT: *The explosion that destroyed the French flagship* L'Orient *in Aboukir Bay on the night of 1 August 1798, a painting by P.-J. de Loutherbourg. The Battle of the Nile 'began at sunset, and was not finished at three the next morning,' Nelson wrote, 'but God favoured our endeavours with a great victory.'*

RIGHT: *'Admiral Nelson recreating with his Brave Tars after the Glorious Battle of the Nile', a print of 1800 commemorating the victory by Thomas Rowlandson. In his despatch, Nelson wrote that the bravery 'of the officers and men of every description was absolutely irresistible'.*

he might emerge with distinction. After 1793, when he already appeared old to the younger generation of officers, he noted carefully his own increasing confidence in battle, the marks of approval gained, the failure of others to acknowledge his efforts and his steady climb in authority. By 1796 the commander-in-chief on the Mediterranean station, Sir John Jervis (later Lord St Vincent), placed Nelson at the top of his list of subordinates he most wanted to keep under his command.

By this time Nelson had realized how important it was for the public and for government ministers to know what he had achieved. Thus, after the Battle of Cape St Vincent, rather than depend on his commander-in-chief's report, published in the *London Gazette*, he wrote his own account for release to the newspapers. He became a deliberate self-publicist.

To some, Nelson's search for acclaim was undignified. Later, even Jervis became irritated by his ostentatious wearing of all his orders and medals for non-ceremonial occasions, even when travelling on shore. But to fleet commanders like Jervis, his hazardous thrusts into the deepest danger, as off Cape St Vincent, were the catalysts of victory.

The ambition that drove Nelson was accompanied by agonizing anxiety. He knew he risked death or mutilation at every hostile encounter. Some thought he was careless with the lives of others as well as with his own. But for him, the challenges could not be ignored. He staked his life, judgement and career against death, which in his profession was a real, ever-present and often imminent reality which always loomed large.

Risk was a prevailing obsession within Nelson's world. The aristocratic, élite class to which he aspired attributed their good fortune to chance. Gambling and duelling gave expression to their fatalistic belief in the rationale for their existence. Nelson thus threw his life into the wheel of chance.

He did so fortified by devout religious faith that came from his upbringing as the son of a country parson who, throughout his life, encouraged Nelson with pious sermons on how to conduct himself. Though he risked all, Nelson placed his fate with God. He came to believe that he led a charmed life and that his decisions were made through divine influence.

As he grew older, and became more famous, he also became more isolated, suffering a

RIGHT: *'The Reward of Courage',
a mezzotint published in 1798 by
J. Fairburn of the French second-
in-command, Admiral Blanquet,
surrendering the French colours to
Nelson after the defeat of the
French fleet at the Battle of the
Nile. Admiral Brueys, the French
commander, was killed in the
explosion of* L'Orient.

ABOVE: *Nelson with the officers and crew of the* Vanguard *at a service of thanksgiving held on the deck of the ship the afternoon after the Battle of the Nile. Nelson wears a bandage over the wound to his forehead.*

good deal from his separation while at sea from those he loved. Yet a sense of public duty, as well as his own conscience, kept him away, and obliged him to accept the responsibilities that were his.

The loss of his mother while a child, and separation from women for long periods, made him, if anything, more emotionally vulnerable than the average man. His open adultery with Emma Hamilton was condemned in his own time, especially by naval colleagues. Yet, at a personal level, he and Emma were clearly highly compatible: both had risen from humble beginnings; they were attracted to one another sexually; and they shared common interests in their relationships with Sir William Hamilton and later in their child, Horatia.

His involvement with Emma and abandonment of his wife brought Nelson into disrepute with George III and respectable society in London. Yet among the general public his moral misdemeanours mattered not at all. To them he remained the national hero his public achievements proclaimed him. Wherever he went, in London, the west of England, Portsmouth, or Germany, curiosity, admiration and affection brought thousands on to the streets.

Seamen in the fleet worshipped him too. He was a commander under whom they developed a confidence and morale that was almost insuperable. Unlike other commanders of his day he treated his seamen with respect as individuals; when he appealed to them not to desert, he talked of their own pride and self-respect as well as of the needs of the country they served.

Most seamen never met or saw him. But they knew of him from others: of his wounds, his irritability, his small size, his manner, the way he wore so many decorations. After the Battle of Trafalgar a seaman recorded:

RIGHT: *Portrait of Nelson painted by the German artist F. G. Füger. He is wearing the Order of St Ferdinand and of Merit, conferred on him by the King of Naples, the Turkish Order of the Crescent and the Order of the Bath.*

ABOVE: *Numerous items, from paper fans and large snufftakers' handkerchiefs to papier-mâché trays and ceramic wares, were produced as mementoes of the nation's hero. This is a Prattware jug of about 1798, with a picture of Captain Berry on the reverse side.*

Our dear Lord Nelson is killed. I never set eyes on him, for which I am both sorry and glad; for to be sure, I should like to have seen him, but all the men in our ship who have seen him have done nothing but curse their eyes and cry. God bless you, chaps that fought like the Devil sit down and cry like a wench.

The writer Robert Southey, noting the impact of news of Nelson's death on shore, wrote:

The death of Nelson was felt in England as something more than a public calamity; men started at the intelligence, and turned pale, as if they had heard of the loss of a dear friend. An object of our admiration and affection, of our pride and of our hopes, was suddenly taken from us; and it seemed as if we had never, till then, known how deeply we loved and reverenced him.

LEFT: *Monument to Nelson at Great Yarmouth on the Norfolk coast. Nelson landed here on his return from Naples, and from here he set sail for the Baltic and the Battle of Copenhagen in 1801.*

RIGHT: *Allegory of 'Fame conducting Admiral Lord Nelson to her Temple', by J. C. Stadler, 1800. A tribute to Nelson's heroism in the classical manner, produced in the year that he returned to England from the Continent after his victory in the eastern Mediterranean.*

CHAPTER ONE

MIDSHIPMAN NELSON

ABOVE: *Nelson's mother, born Catherine Suckling, before her marriage to Edmund Nelson. Horatio was the third of her eight children to survive. He was nine when she died in 1767.*

NELSON WAS BORN ON 29 September 1758. He was the son of Edmund Nelson, Rector of Burnham Thorpe, in Norfolk, and of his wife Catherine, daughter of Dr Suckling, Prebendary of Westminster; her grandmother was sister to Sir Robert Walpole, prime minister in the second quarter of the eighteenth century, as noted by Nelson in the only account that he wrote of himself. The rector and his family were not of sufficient standing to be invited to Houghton Hall, the nearby Walpole seat. Moreover, Edmund Nelson, the son of a Cambridge baker, was not someone who impressed his social superiors, being 'tremulous over trifles and easily put in "a fuss" '.

Edmund was conscious of his lack of social standing and of confidence, and Nelson was to suffer from a similar sense of his inadequacies, for which he felt some need to compensate. He also inherited his father's tendency to anxiety and fussiness over details, together with a dutiful regard for the will of God that was to be a comfort to him throughout his life.

Nelson's idea of what was possible with ambition and determination came from his mother. Catherine was a practical woman, forthright in her hatred of England's traditional enemy, the French, and fulsome in her adulation of sea officers. At the time of Nelson's birth her elder brother, Captain Maurice Suckling, was fighting in a successful naval engagement with the French in the Caribbean and was thereafter the family hero. Suckling's career revealed for Nelson a passage to fame and social position for even a boy of relatively humble origins. Nelson was nine when his mother died in 1767. In his mid-forties, his love for her was undiminished: 'the thought of former days brings all my mother to my heart, which shows itself in my eyes'.

ABOVE: *Rev. Edmund Nelson, painted in old age by Sir William Beechey. The early influence of his father was to remain with Nelson throughout his life.*

RIGHT: *All Saints church, Burnham Thorpe, Norfolk, by M. E. Cotman. Edmund Nelson was Rector of Burnham Thorpe.*

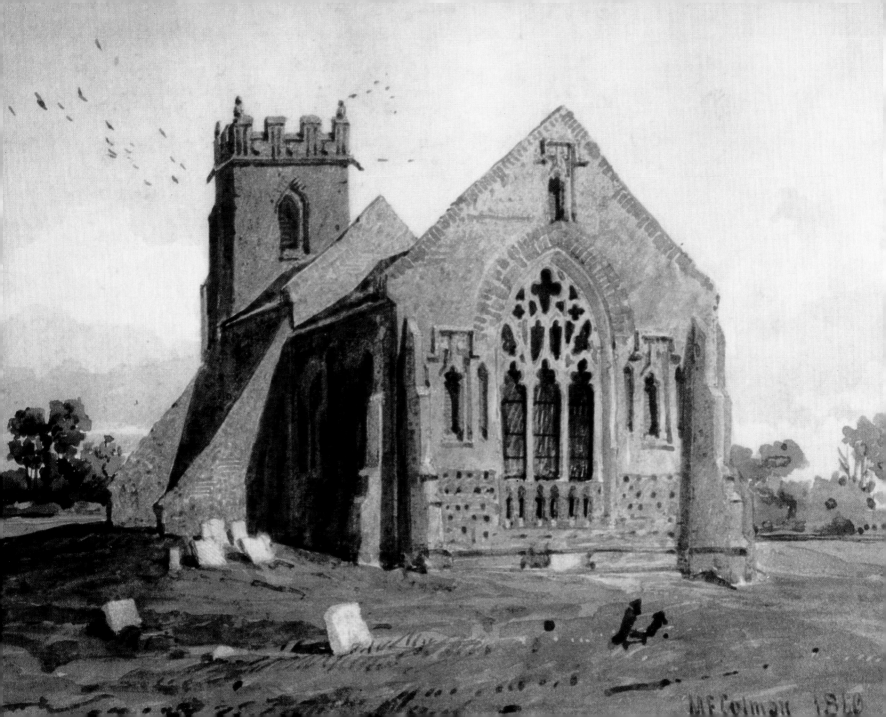

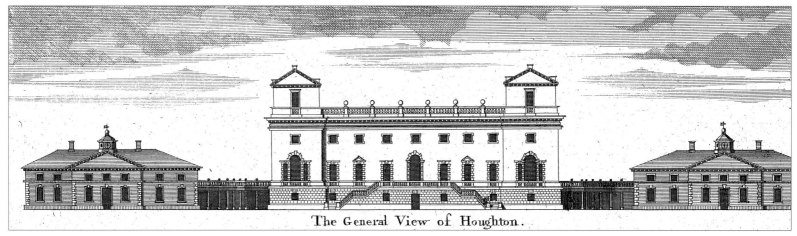

The General View of Houghton.

ABOVE: *Houghton Hall, Norfolk, the family seat of the Walpoles, to whom Nelson's mother was distantly related: her grandmother was sister to Sir Robert Walpole, George I's prime minister.*

Catherine Nelson bore her husband eleven children, of whom three girls and five boys survived. Horace, or Horatio, as he preferred to call himself, was the third boy. He was known in the family for his 'spirit': for his ability to master one of his elder brothers in a fight; for his determination to get to school through snowdrifts in spite of the reluctance of his brother William; for his daring in raiding the headmaster's orchard and then involving his less adventurous peers by giving them the fruit to eat. For such a boy, in such a family, the loss of his mother acted as an incentive to take his place in the world and to succeed.

Initially Nelson was sent with his elder brothers to the Royal Grammar School at Norwich, a cathedral school where the boys boarded during term-time. In 1768, following his mother's death, Nelson was removed, first to Downham Market, then to Sir William Paston's School, in North Walsham. When he and William returned for the Christmas holiday in 1770, they found their father had temporarily escaped the winter 'wind and storm and rattling hail' to more comfortable lodgings in Bath. At the same time naval mobilization over Spanish claims to the Falkland Islands had given their uncle, Maurice Suckling, command of a 64-gun ship, the *Raisonnable*, fitting out at Chatham. Nelson immediately appealed to William to write to their father, to ask

Suckling to take him into his ship. Edmund did so, and Suckling good-humouredly accepted responsibility for his unlikely nephew:

> What has poor Horace done, who is so weak that he, above all the rest, should
> be sent to rough it at sea? But let him come and the first time we go into
> action a cannon-ball may knock off his head and provide for him at once.

Nelson was then 12. Later he was to observe that a boy who went to sea at a similar age was 'much too young'. His own first day on the *Raisonnable* off Chatham in the River Medway, early in March 1771, was desolate. Suckling was absent; Nelson was not expected, and ignored; the ship was swept by 'fresh gales with squally weather and snow'; and he was berthed in the darkness of the orlop deck beneath the waterline where midshipmen had their quarters.

BELOW: *Sir William Paston's School, North Walsham, a small private school attended by Nelson from 1768 to 1771.*

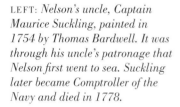

LEFT: *Nelson's uncle, Captain Maurice Suckling, painted in 1754 by Thomas Bardwell. It was through his uncle's patronage that Nelson first went to sea. Suckling later became Comptroller of the Navy and died in 1778.*

RIGHT: *'A Midshipman with a Longboat', from a series of prints of naval officers' dress by Dominic Serres, 1777. Through his uncle's influence, Nelson joined the* Raisonnable *as a midshipman in 1771, at the age of 12.*

Over the next few weeks the ship had to be fitted, rigged, stored and gunned, and manoeuvred down the Medway to Sheerness. Yet, as he wrote later, his career soon took an unexpected turn:

> the business with Spain being accommodated, I was sent in a West India ship belonging to the house of Hibbert, Purrier and Horton, with Mr John Rathbone who had formerly been in the navy, in the *Dreadnought* with Captain Suckling.

Before a midshipman could qualify as a lieutenant, he had to have had at least six years' service at sea and to have attained 20 years of age. Suckling certainly knew that service in a merchant trading vessel was far better experience than that in the stationary ship in which he himself was serving; for in May 1771 Suckling had been transferred to the *Triumph*, the guardship at the Nore in the mouth of the Thames.

It was to this ship that Nelson returned in 1772, imbued with the prejudices of the merchant seaman against the Royal Navy – hatred of impressment, of flogging, and of the petty tyrannies of martinet officers who demanded 'smart' ships to win the praise of their superiors:

> If I did not improve in my education, I returned a practical seaman with a horror of the Royal Navy, and with a saying then constant with the seaman, 'Aft the most honour, forward the better man!'.

BELOW: *Portrait miniature, believed to be of Nelson at the age of eight. This would have been before his mother died and while he was at the Royal Grammar School in Norwich.*

ABOVE: *Chatham Dockyard, an illustration from* A Prospect of Great Britain *by Samuel and Nathaniel Buck. In the Thames and Medway Nelson learnt to navigate in shallow waters, experience that was later to stand him in good stead.*

It was, as he recalled, many weeks before he again became reconciled to a warship, 'so deep was the prejudice rooted':

> However, as my ambition was to be a seaman, it was always held out as a reward that, if I attended well to my navigation, I should go in the cutter and decked long-boat, which was attached to the commanding officer's ship at Chatham. Thus by degrees I became a good pilot for vessels of that description, from Chatham to the Tower of London, down the Swin and to the North Foreland; and confident of myself amongst rocks and sands, which has many times since been of the very greatest comfort to me.

This confidence in shallow waters was to become part of Nelson's seafaring acumen. In the French wars the inshore blockade of enemy naval bases and seizure of enemy coasting vessels all demanded skill in such circumstances:

> In this way I was trained till the expedition towards the North Pole was fitted out; when, although no boys were allowed to go in the ships (as of no use), yet nothing

could prevent my using every interest to go with Captain Lutwidge in the *Carcass*; and, as I fancied I was to fill a man's place, I begged I might be his cockswain; which, finding my ardent desire for going with him, Captain Lutwidge complied with and has continued the strictest friendship to this moment.

No doubt Nelson saw the *Racehorse* and *Carcass* fitting out for their Arctic voyage on one of his passages up the Thames from Chatham. Suckling was a friend of the First Lord of the Admiralty, Lord Sandwich, and it was probably through him that Nelson was accepted into the *Carcass*.

The expedition up the west coast of Spitzbergen was in search of a northern waterway stretching to the east, which might provide a route to the China Sea and the Pacific. Early in August 1773 the two ships became stuck in the ice. Their crews were unable to cut their way out, and it was decided to drag the boats to the water's edge. Nelson aspired to a command:

> When the boats were fitted out to quit the two ships blocked up in the ice, I exerted myself to have the command of a four-oared cutter raised upon [me], which was given me, with twelve men; and I prided myself in fancying I could navigate her better than any other boat in the ship.

After the men had dragged the boats for three miles, however, the wind changed direction and the ice opened up, allowing the ships to escape.

It was on this voyage that Nelson, with a young collaborator, attempted to obtain a polar bear's skin for his father. Having ventured forth in the middle of the night, they found a bear. But their musket misfired and Nelson's companion made off. Nelson hoped to 'get a blow' at the bear with the butt of the musket but was divided from the beast by a chasm in the ice. His absence being noticed on board the *Carcass*, a gun was fired from the ship which scared the bear off. Though Nelson was reprimanded on his return, his energy and enthusiasm gained the approval of the officers of the two ships, including Captain the Hon. Constantine Phipps, later Lord Mulgrave, who commanded the *Racehorse* and the whole expedition. Suckling was obviously pleased with reports of his conduct for, on Nelson's return, he quickly found him another berth in a ship destined for the East Indies:

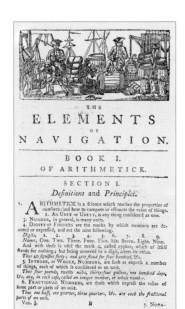

ABOVE: *Page from J. Robertson's* The Elements of Navigation, *6th edition, 1796, a manual of the type used by midshipmen in the latter part of the eighteenth century.*

LEFT: *The* Racehorse *and the* Carcass *trapped in the Arctic ice on 7 August 1773. An engraving based on sketches by Midshipman Philippe d'Auvergne, who took part in the expedition to find a new sea route to China and the Pacific.*

ABOVE: *Thomas Stothard's patriotic frontispiece to Frederic Hervey's* Naval History of Great Britain, *1779. 'A sudden glow of patriotism was kindled' within Nelson on board the* Dolphin.

> I was placed in the *Seahorse* of 20 guns, with Captain Farmer, and watched in the foretop, from whence in time I was placed on the quarter-deck: having, in the time I was in this ship, visited almost every part of the East-Indies, from Bengal to Bussorah. Ill-health induced Sir Edward Hughes, who had always shown me the greatest kindness, to send me to England in the *Dolphin* of 20 guns.

Nelson's ill health was caused by malaria. At Bombay at the end of 1775 he was so ill that he was not expected to live. He continued to be ill on the voyage home but fortunately had the benefit of a month's rest off Simonstown near the Cape of Good Hope. He remained weak and depressed, but on the slow haul north through the south Atlantic he had a spiritual experience: the vision of a 'radiant orb' combined with a sudden sense of personal dedication that would accompany him for the rest of his life:

> I felt impressed with a feeling that I should never rise in my profession. My mind was staggered with a view of the difficulties I had to surmount and the

ABOVE: *'Nelson and the Bear', a print of 1806 from Edward Orme's* Graphic History of the Life of Nelson. *A direct confrontation was broken off when the bear was frightened away by a shot fired from the* Carcass.

little interest I possessed. I could discover no means of reaching the object of my ambition. After a long and gloomy reverie, in which I almost wished myself overboard, a sudden glow of patriotism was kindled within me and presented my King and Country as my patron. Well then, I will be a hero and, confiding in Providence, I will brave every danger.

Nelson need not have felt despondent, for by the time of his return his uncle had been made Comptroller of the Navy, the chairman of the Navy Board which, beneath the Board of Admiralty, administered the dockyards and made most of the warrant officers' appointments throughout the Navy. War with Great Britain's rebellious American colonies had finally broken out, and there was no want of employment for a young man with 'interest'.

Almost within hours of being paid off from the *Dolphin* in September 1776, Nelson was issued with an appointment as acting lieutenant on board the *Worcester* of 64 guns. Furthermore, with his uncle as Comptroller, he himself now had influence and could, through his own observations or complaints, make or break the career of his new commanding officer, Captain Robinson. The latter thus had every reason to give Nelson encouragement, entrusting him with a watch, in spite of bad weather, as the *Worcester* convoyed merchant vessels to and from Gibraltar and into the North Sea.

Although still only 18, not 20 – as his passing certificate afterwards declared him to be – Nelson was examined for lieutenant a week after the *Worcester* returned to Portsmouth. Suckling was a member of the examining board but did not disclose his relationship with the candidate. Only after Nelson had provided 'prompt and satisfactory' answers to the questions did he rise and introduce his nephew to the other captains. Entry into the rank of lieutenant remained dependent on receiving a commission to a ship but, again, Suckling allowed no time to elapse before a ship was found for him.

ABOVE: *Captain William Locker, a portrait by Gilbert Stuart. Nelson admired the older officer and kept up a regular correspondence with him. 'Our friendship will never end but with my life', Nelson wrote, but in the event Locker died before Nelson.*

RIGHT: *Richard Westall's painting of Lieutenant Nelson responding to the words of the captain of the* Lowestoffe, *'Have I no officer in the ship who can board the prize?' The incident, related in Nelson's own account of his early life, occurred in 1777.*

On [9] April 1777 I passed my examination as lieutenant; and received my commission the next day as second lieutenant of the *Lowestoffe* frigate of 32 guns, Captain ... William Locker. In this ship I went to Jamaica; but even a frigate was not sufficiently active for my mind, and I got into a schooner, tender to the *Lowestoffe*. In this vessel I made myself a complete pilot for all the passages through the [Keys] islands situated on the north side [of] Hispaniola.

Although Nelson now thought himself 'left in [the] world to shift for myself', Suckling's influence went with him even to the Caribbean. For a while he was placed in command of the schooner – renamed *Little Lucy* by Locker after his daughter – to gain experience as an independent commander, and on his first voyage he took a prize, an American schooner, after an eight-hour chase:

Whilst in this frigate [the *Lowestoffe*], an event happened which presaged my character; and as it conveys no dishonour to the officer alluded to, I shall relate it. Blowing a gale of wind, and very heavy sea, the frigate captured an American letter of marque. The first lieutenant was ordered to board her, which he did not do, owing to the very heavy sea. On his return, the Captain said, 'Have I no officer in the ship who can board the prize?' On which the Master ran to the gangway to get into the boat, when I stopped him, saying 'It is my turn now; and if I come back, it is yours'. This little incident has often occurred to my mind; and I know it is my disposition that difficulties and dangers do but increase my desire of attempting them.

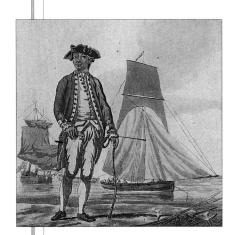

ABOVE: *'A Lieutenant with a Cutter' by Dominic Serres, 1777. Nelson passed the examination for lieutenant in that year and joined Locker's ship the* Lowestoffe.

While the *Lowestoffe* was off Jamaica, Sir Peter Parker, the commander-in-chief on the station, arrived. He too was conscious of the value of Suckling's favour. In 1778, soon after his arrival, Parker took Nelson into his own flagship, the *Bristol*, as third lieutenant. From this position he rose, as Parker intended, to be first lieutenant.

France had declared war early in February 1778, bringing Great Britain into conflict within Europe as well as with her American colonies. The seizure of many prizes and an increase in the number of ships that Britain needed in commission soon gave Nelson an opportunity for an independent command. On 8 December 1778, after brief service in the *Bristol*:

> I was appointed commander of the *Badger* brig; and was first sent to protect the Mosquito shore and the Bay of Honduras from the depredations of the American privateers. Whilst on this service, I gained so much the affections of the settlers that they unanimously voted me their thanks, and expressed their regret on my leaving them.

Later, while anchored in Montego Bay on the north coast of Jamaica, he helped to avert a tragedy by taking on board the crew of the *Glasgow*, which was on fire.

ABOVE: *An eighteenth-century view of the town and harbour of Montego Bay, Jamaica, where Nelson anchored with the* Badger *and took on board the crew of the* Glasgow, *on which a fire had broken out.*

In June 1778 Suckling died. As well as patronage, he had provided Nelson with advice, in 1777, for example, he sent him a letter instructing him in the rules that are necessary for keeping a ship 'in very high order'. Nelson now depended for advancement on his own reputation.

In addition to proving his ability during this period, Nelson had been making friends. Among them was Cuthbert Collingwood, who replaced him in the *Lowestoffe*. His closest friendship, however, was with William Locker. In the Caribbean Locker's health was not good, and as early as August 1777 Nelson offered to take care of his effects should he die. After Locker departed for London in July 1779, their friendship continued in correspondence, until Locker's death in 1800. Nelson confessed to owing him a great deal and later wrote:

> I have been your scholar; it is you who taught me to board a Frenchman ... It is you who always told me 'Lay a Frenchman close and you will beat him'; and my only merit in my profession is being a good scholar.

This was a lesson Nelson now had the opportunity to apply. For on 11 June 1779, on his return from Montego Bay with the crew of the *Glasgow*, he heard he had been 'made post' as captain of the frigate *Hinchinbrooke*.

CHAPTER TWO

'THE MEREST BOY
OF A CAPTAIN'

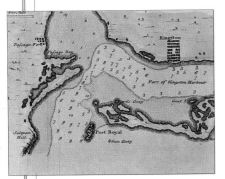

ABOVE: *Port Royal, Jamaica,
shown on a map of about 1760.
Nelson was put in command of the
batteries at Port Royal at a time
when an attack by the French
was expected.*

N ELSON WAS 20 WHEN HE was appointed captain of the *Hinchinbrooke*, a
28-gun frigate. In spite of his youth, he now had authority over about
170 men and was placed on the established list of captains upon which
he could rise by seniority to become an admiral. Temporarily, however, the
frigate was delayed at sea, possibly even captured, and Nelson was called upon
to perform military duties on shore. Jamaica was then at the very heart of the
strategic conflict between France and Britain, for the French were intent on
seizing the British sugar islands. In August 1779 the French admiral, Count
d'Estaing, was reported to have arrived in the Caribbean with nearly 30 ships
of the line, nearly 100 troop transports and the opportunity to embark 25,000
men from Martinique:

RIGHT: *Roaring River estate,
a Jamaican sugar plantation.
Roaring River belonged
to William Beckford, with
whom Nelson was later to
stay in England.*

> An attack on Jamaica was expected. In this critical state, I was ... entrusted with
> the command of the batteries at Port Royal; and I need not say, as the defence
> of this place was the key to the port of the whole naval force, the town of
> Kingston, and Spanish Town, it was the most important post in the whole island.

Nelson had every right to feel pride in the trust placed in him. He was given
charge of 500 men in Fort Charles, one of the batteries commanding the harbour at Port Royal, while another 6,000 were camped around Kingston and in
other forts. But the French did not come after all, and in September the
Hinchinbrooke arrived safely at Port Royal.

War was declared against Spain in 1779, and Nelson resumed his patrol of
the coast of Central America until December. On his return to Jamaica the
Governor, Major-General Dalling, confided in Nelson his plan to cut the

Spanish colonies in Central America in two by driving an expedition into Nicaragua up the River San Juan and across Lake Nicaragua to the city of Granada, itself within striking distance of the Pacific coast. The only obstacle appeared to be the Spanish fort of San Juan, situated some 65 miles up the river. He had put the scheme to Lord George Germain, the Secretary for the Colonies in London, and received encouragement. Nelson too was encouraging, perhaps recognizing a scheme by which to advance himself. However, Admiral Parker was not enthusiastic: he was short of ships and equipment, aware of the dangers of disease to large bodies of men operating in tropical jungle and sceptical of the advantage to be gained from the expedition. Nevertheless he did not object to Dalling's employment of Nelson, with his knowledge of the coastline:

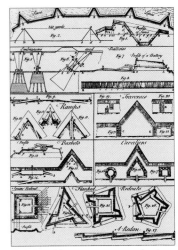

ABOVE: *The construction of a fort, a page from a treatise on the subject in Robertson's* The Elements of Navigation.

BELOW: Sketch, believed to be of Nelson planning an attack on a fort. On the plan is written, 'The first line to advance. The second will support.'

In January 1780, an expedition being resolved on against St Juan's, I was chosen to command the sea part of it. Major Polson, who commanded, will tell you of my exertions: how I quitted my ship, carried troops in boats one hundred miles up a river, which none but Spaniards since the time of the buccaneers had ever ascended. It will then be told how I boarded, if I may be allowed the expression, an outpost of the enemy, situated on an island in the river.

Polson recalled that 'a light-haired boy came to me in a little frigate, of whom I at first made little account'. After delays in attempts to recruit pilots and reinforcements from coastal settlements, the convoy reached the mouth of the San Juan river safely under Nelson's supervision. Once there the troops were temporarily camped on a swampy shore, where they were vulnerable to mosquitoes, while stores and equipment were reloaded into a collection of small craft. These included local canoes which, upon setting out, proved top-heavy or unnavigable. Though Nelson's official duty was done, he employed two of the *Hinchinbrooke's* boats and 50 seamen and marines in reloading and navigating the vessels up-river.

His professional assistance achieved the desired result. After two weeks, in spite of groundings, tropical rainstorms,

LEFT: *An eighteenth-century view of Portsmouth with shipping in the Solent beyond. Nelson landed at Portsmouth from Jamaica in 1780, weakened by malaria and dysentery.*

and all the frights and frustrations of navigating through rain forest, the boats reached the fortress of San Juan. A protective island battery was taken by surprise at night and siege was laid to the fortress, Nelson landing four small cannon and aiming the guns. Almost immediately he was seized with stomach pains, and over the next two weeks succumbed to dysentery and malaria. The second wave of British troops arrived and was on the point of attacking the fort as Nelson was sent by canoe down river to the coast, in a desperate attempt to save his life.

At the mouth of the San Juan river at the beginning of May 1780 Nelson handed over command of the *Hinchinbrooke* to Collingwood and made his way to Jamaica. He had been appointed to the *Janus*, a larger frigate, but was too ill to go to sea. At Kingston he recuperated, spending part of the time at the house of Admiral Parker. But recovery was slow and lonely. One desolate letter recorded, 'Lady P. not here, the servants letting me lay as if a log, and take no notice'. Eventually he gave up hope of commanding the *Janus* and in September, with Admiralty permission, took passage for London.

I return to England hope revives within me [he informed an acquaintance, Hercules Ross]. I shall recover and my dream of glory be fulfilled. Nelson will yet be an Admiral. It is the climate that has destroyed my health and crushed my spirit. Home and dear friends will restore me.

He landed at Portsmouth in December but still remained weak. From Bath in January 1781, he wrote to Locker:

ABOVE: *The parsonage house at Burnham Thorpe, where Nelson was born. He returned here after his tours of duty in the West Indies.*

I have been so ill since I have been here that I was obliged to be carried to and from bed with the most excruciating tortures but, thank God, I am now upon the mending hand. I [am] physicked three times a day, drink the waters three times, and bathe every other night, besides [not] drinking wine, which I think the worst of all ... as you will suppose, I do not set under the hands of a doctor very easy, although I give myself credit this once for having done everything, and taken every medicine that was ordered, that Dr Woodward, who is my physician, said he never had a better patient ... Although I have not quite recovered the use of my limbs, yet my inside is a new man; and I have no doubt but in two or three weeks I shall be perfectly well ...

RIGHT: *John Francis Rigaud's portrait, begun when Nelson was a lieutenant and completed in 1781. At this date the uniform was changed to show him as a captain, the hat originally held under his left arm was put on his head and the fortress of San Juan was painted into the background.*

And indeed he did continue to recover, though more slowly than he expected. In mid-February he was able to tell Locker:

My health, thank God, is very near perfectly restored; and I have the perfect use of all my limbs except my left arm, which I can hardly tell what is the matter with it. From the shoulder to my fingers' ends are as if half dead ...

Medicine At Sea

THE CAPTAIN AND LIEUTENANTS of a ship were expected to ensure seamen had an appropriate diet, suitable clothing and that they kept clean. Seamen who fell ill were the responsibility of the ship's surgeon. In 1793 there were 550 surgeons in the Royal Navy; by 1806, 720. They held university degrees and had been examined by the Court of Examiners of the Company of Surgeons before receiving a warrant of appointment from the Navy Board.

Most of the time surgeons dealt with minor ailments: seasickness afflicted many men at the outset of a voyage, for which 'a draught or two' of sea water was recommended, or a teaspoonful of 'aether' in a glass of water. Intoxication was also frequently treated.

For treating feverishness and other ailments the surgeon was equipped at the outset of a voyage with various pharmaceutical commodities. These included Peruvian bark, purging salts, blistering plaster, sarsaparilla, camomile flowers or hops, senna leaves, linseed, conserve of roses, whole mustard seed, manna, nitre, laudanum, myrrh, crude mercury and opium.

The surgeon was able to perform on board every form of surgery arising from wounds, ulcers and accidents. He carried with him amputating knives, both single- and double-edged, an amputating saw and a metacarpal saw, forceps for arteries and larger parts of the body, curved needles, screw tourniquets, bone nippers, trephines for

LEFT: *The wounded lying among marksmen on the upper deck of the Victory at Trafalgar. The men caught in enemy fire would be carried below to receive medical attention.*

cranial surgery, scalpels, probes, lancets and a scoop for extracting gun shots. His medicine chest would also have contained apparatus for 'cupping' and 'blistering', trusses, splints, bandages, cloth and tape, and a key for extracting teeth by torsion. Most of the instruments were made of iron or steel, and some had bone handles.

On the orlop deck, a space was cleared among the ship's cables.

Let there be a fixed chest of proper height to perform your operations upon, and on another just by lay all your apparatus ... Also a bucket of water to put your sponges in, and another empty to receive the blood in your operations; a dry swab or two to dry the platform when necessary; a water cask full of water near at hand in readiness for dipping out occasionally.

Amputation was the operation most frequently performed. The surgeon had 'to acquire an expertness in using the ligature and tenaculum' – a sharp hook used for picking up arteries – and, in the absence of anaesthetics, work with speed and decisiveness.

ABOVE: *Surgeon's mahogany medicine chest, with drawers and bottles for the ship's supply of powders, essences and balms. This one belonged to Sir Benjamin Outram, who served at the Battle of Copenhagen.*

RIGHT AND BELOW: *Instruments carried by a ship's surgeon. A boy named Samuel Leech described finding the ship's surgeon and his mate in their civilian clothes, 'smeared with blood from head to foot'. He held one of his messmates 'while the surgeon cut off his leg above the knee. The task was most painful to behold, the surgeon using his knife and saw on human flesh as freely as the butcher at the shambles.'*

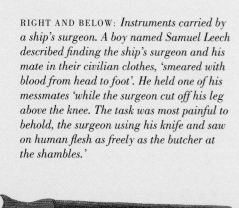

but the surgeons and doctors give me hopes it will all go off. I most sincerely wish to be employed, and hope it will not be long.

In this hope, in March he travelled by stages to London, only to have a relapse, attended with a slight fever. In May, he was still complaining of the loss of use of his left arm, left leg and thigh. It was therefore probably fortunate that Lord Sandwich, the First Lord of the Admiralty, 'could fix no time' when he should be employed, although he promised he would employ him at 'the first opportunity'.

Recuperation on half pay allowed Nelson time to stay with his uncle and brothers, to visit Burnham Thorpe and to have a portrait completed – begun by John Francis Rigaud before he left for the West Indies as a lieutenant four years earlier, in 1777. Then he had been a plump-featured young teenager – 'not in the least like' he was now. Consequently, on his return to Rigaud's studio in 1781, the portrait was altered: the face made thinner, the uniform brought up to date, the hat placed authoritatively on the head rather than under the arm, and the fort of San Juan added in the background.

> In August 1781, I was commissioned for the *Albemarle*; and, it would almost be supposed, to try my constitution, was kept the whole winter in the North Sea.

Nelson was 'perfectly satisfied' with the *Albemarle*, a 28-gun frigate, which he found being coppered and refitted in dock at Woolwich. Lord Sandwich allowed him to choose all his own officers, and he was able to recruit some volunteer seamen – 'as good a set of men as I ever saw'. His marines were 'likewise old standers'. But he had to make up his crew by seizing men from an East Indiaman returning into the Thames estuary, a chase that demanded the expenditure of 26 nine-pounder and one 18-pounder shot.

All these exertions took their toll. By the time the *Albemarle* arrived at the Nore on 21 October, Nelson had become 'so ill, as hardly [to be] kept out of bed'. Yet his instructions directed him to take two other frigates under his command and escort a convoy of merchant ships from the Baltic back to the English coast. Off Helsingör Castle it was so cold he almost 'froze'; back off Yarmouth just before Christmas, it felt 'quite summer'.

ABOVE: *'Sailors', an illustration from John Augustus Atkinson's* Costume of Britain, *1808, showing the trousers, breeches and neckerchiefs worn by seamen at this period. Trained seamen were liable to be impressed into the navy in wartime to meet manning levels.*

RIGHT: *'Heaving the lead'. Atkinson's print of an able seaman taking soundings to gauge the depth of water. Nelson was renowned for the care he took of his men, at one time writing to the Navy Board to recommend that they were issued with longer Guernsey jackets.*

Some of the merchantmen were storeships carrying vital naval stores – timber, tar and hemp – that had to be escorted to the dockyards at Portsmouth and Plymouth. The main threat was from the Dutch, who had entered the American War in 1780. But they missed their opportunity. 'What fools the Dutch must have been not to have taken us into the Texel. Two hundred and sixty sail the convoy consisted of.' Moreover, 'they behaved as all convoys that ever I saw did, shamefully ill, parting company every day'.

Then, ordered to Portsmouth with some outward-bound East Indiamen and to reprovision the *Albemarle*, the frigate was badly damaged by an East Indiaman that drove from her anchors in a hard gale. The frigate had to be docked. Nelson was still in Portsmouth in March when General Dalling returned from Jamaica. It was then, perhaps, that he learned how little had been achieved on the San Juan expedition except the expenditure of many lives and much equipment.

In April 1782 Nelson sailed with a convoy for Newfoundland and Quebec. Eager for prizes, he remained at Quebec only three days before setting out in search of enemy traders and privateers. Early in the voyage he captured an American fishing schooner and took the seaman in command, Nathaniel Carver, on board as a pilot. It was due to Carver's sailing directions that Nelson was able to escape three French ships of the line and then challenge the French frigate *Iris* in shallow waters. In gratitude, Nelson released Carver and his ship. The crew of the *Albemarle* returned into the St Lawrence estuary 'knocked up with scurvy': Nelson and the other officers had lived on salt beef for eight weeks, while the seamen had not had fresh food for more than five months.

On shore at Quebec, Nelson fell in love. Mary Simpson, the object of his affection, was 16 years old; Nelson himself was 24. Mary recalled him as 'erect

ABOVE: *In 1782 Nelson set sail for Newfoundland and Quebec, as captain of the* Albemarle. *'In the end, our cruise has been an unsuccessful one,' he was to write; 'we have taken, seen, and destroyed more enemies than is seldom done in the same space of time, but not one arrived in port.'*

and stern of aspect', a consequence, no doubt, of having to converse with her father, Colonel Saunders Simpson, Provost-Marshal of the garrison, whenever he called. Their courtship lasted no more than eight weeks, for at the beginning of October orders were received at Quebec for troop transports to be fitted and sent to New York. Nelson was instructed to convoy them there, 'a very *pretty job* at this late season of the year, for our sails are at this moment frozen to the yards'. On the point of departure he determined on a proposal of marriage, telling his friend Alexander Davison, 'I find it utterly impossible to leave this place without waiting on her whose society has so much added to its charms and laying myself and my fortunes at her feet.' Davison, eight years older and convinced that this was mere infatuation, advised, 'Your utter ruin, situated as you are at present, must inevitably follow.' Nelson, fixed in his course, responded, 'Then let it follow, for I am resolved to do it.' In the end, Nelson gave way and returned to his ship.

Romance and a touch of the cold autumnal air of Quebec seem to have had a beneficial effect on Nelson for at last he threw off the ill effects of Nicaragua. 'Health, that greatest of blessings, is what I never truly enjoyed till I saw *Fair Canada*,' he wrote to his father. 'The change it has wrought, I am convinced, is truly wonderful.' Optimism about his future had also returned with his health. 'My interest at home you know is next to nothing,' he wrote to a friend, 'the name of Nelson being little known. It may be different one of these days; a good chance only is wanting to make it so.'

From Quebec he sailed with the convoy to New York where, on the look-out once more for patrons, he waited on Lord Hood, a friend of his uncle. Later, on board Hood's flagship, he was noticed by Prince William, third son of George III, then a midshipman. To the Prince, himself only 17, Nelson appeared:

The merest boy of a captain I ever beheld, and his dress was worthy of attention. He had on a full-laced uniform; his lank unpowdered hair was tied in a stiff hessian tail, of an extraordinary length; the old-fashioned flaps of his waistcoat added to the general quaintness of his figure, and produced an appearance which particularly attracted my notice, for I had never seen anything like it before, nor could I imagine who he was, nor what he came about. My doubts were, however, removed, when Lord Hood introduced me to him. There was something irresistibly pleasing in his address and conversation; and an enthusiasm when speaking on professional subjects that showed he was no common being.

Nelson's curious appearance and his professional enthusiasm was something that many would notice during his career.

Hood and Prince William seemed to make much of him, and Nelson responded by doting on the Prince. In late February he wrote to Locker in the vain and deferential manner that was becoming characteristic:

LEFT: *Pierced island, in the Gulf of St Lawrence. From the St Lawrence, Nelson wrote to his father on 19 October 1782, 'We sail with a fleet for New York tomorrow ... but in our line of life we are sure of no one thing.'*

My situation in Lord Hood's fleet must be in the highest degree flattering to any young man. He treats me as if I was his son, and will, I am convinced give me anything I can ask of him; nor is my situation with Prince William less flattering. Lord Hood was so kind as to tell him (indeed I cannot make use of expressions strong enough to describe what I felt) that if he wished to ask questions relative to naval tactics, I could give him as much information as any officer in the fleet. He will be, I am certain, an ornament to our service. He is a *seaman*, which you could hardly suppose. Every other qualification you may expect from him. But he will be a *disciplinarian*, and a strong one: he says he is determined every person shall serve his time before they shall be provided for, as he is obliged to serve his.

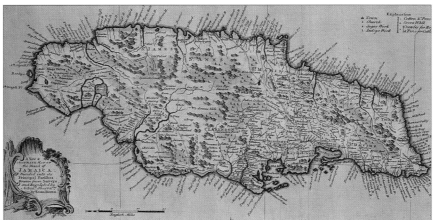

LEFT: *Map of Jamaica dating from about 1760. After its capture in 1655, Jamaica became Britain's richest possession and principal base in the West Indies.*

However, Nelson's enthusiasm was not as yet matched by professional experience and sound judgement. The main fleet, including the *Albemarle*, sailed south for Jamaica in February 1783. *En route* and on his own initiative, Nelson, in company with several other vessels, attempted to remove a small garrison of French soldiers from Turks Island at the south-eastern end of the Bahamas. But his summons to surrender was refused and his direct assault was driven off. After withdrawing and bombarding the fort from a distance, Nelson was forced to sail away and report his failure.

Nevertheless Hood seemed not to think the worse of him for it. The preliminaries of peace having been signed, Nelson was despatched with Prince William to make a two-day good-will visit to Havana in Cuba, before returning to England, where the *Albemarle* was paid off. In July Hood rewarded Nelson for looking after the Prince by taking him to St James's to meet the King, who was 'exceedingly attentive'. He also visited Windsor to take leave of the Prince, who was embarking on a tour of Europe. Otherwise, as he told Locker:

> My time ever since I arrived in Town has been taken up in attempting to get
> the wages due to my *good fellows*, for various ships they have served in the
> war. The disgust of the seamen to the navy is all owing the infernal plan of

turning them over from ship to ship, so that men cannot be attached to their officers, or the officers care two-pence about them. My ship was paid off last week, and in such a manner that must flatter any officer, in particular in these turbulent times. The whole ship's company offered, if I could get a ship, to enter for her immediately; but I have no thought of going to sea, for I cannot afford to live on board ship, in such a manner as is going on at present.

RIGHT: *Prince William (left), wearing a midshipman's uniform, with the younger Prince Edward, painted by Benjamin West in 1778. Nelson told Locker that the Prince's temper and good sense was bound to be 'pleasing to everyone ... In every respect, both as a man and a prince, I love him.'*

Instead, like Prince William, Nelson decided to extend his experience by going to the Continent to improve his French. In October, with Captain James Macnamara, he crossed from Dover to Calais and travelled *en poste* to Marquise, and thence to Montreuil, Boulogne, Abbeville and St Omer. His first impressions of France were not favourable:

I was highly diverted by looking what a curious figure the postillions in their jack boots and their rats of horses made together. Their chaises have no springs, and the roads generally paved like London streets; therefore you will naturally suppose we were pretty well shook together by the time we had travelled two posts and a half, which is fifteen miles, to Marquise. Here we [were] shown into an inn – they called it – I should have called it a pigstye; we were shown into a room with two straw beds, and, with great difficulty, they mustered up clean sheets; and gave us two pigeons for supper, upon a dirty cloth, and wooden-handled knives – *Oh what a transition from happy England.* But we laughed at the repast, and went to bed with determination that nothing should ruffle our tempers.

This was France prior to the Revolution. At Boulogne he could not help observing that 'neither good lodgings or

ABOVE: *The customs house at Boulogne, a watercolour drawing by Thomas Rowlandson. 'We set off at daylight for Boulogne, where we breakfasted,' reported Nelson to Locker; 'this place was full of English, I suppose because wine is so very cheap.'*

master could be had, for there are no middling class of people: sixty noblemen's families lived in the town, who owned the vast plain round it, and the rest very poor indeed.' At St Omer he and 'Mac' took lodgings with a 'pleasant French family'. There, two 'very agreeable' daughters often kept them company, made their breakfasts and played cards with them in the evenings. 'Therefore I must learn French if 'tis only for the pleasure of talking to them, for they do not speak a word of English.'

However, a week later these pleasures were eclipsed when Nelson dined with an English clergyman named Andrews who had two 'very beautiful young ladies'. They played music and sang for their visitors. Three weeks later Nelson had become quite attached to one of them. As he told his brother:

My heart is quite secured against the French beauties: I almost wish I could say as much for an English young lady, the daughter of a clergyman, with whom I am just going to dine and spend the day. She has such accomplishments that had I a million of money I am sure I should at this moment make her an offer of them: my income at present is by far too small to think of marriage, and she has no fortune.

At the beginning of January Nelson was still having tea and spending the evening 'with the most accomplished woman' his eyes had ever beheld. Indeed, by the middle of January 1784, his emotions perhaps affected by news of the death of his sister Anne, he had decided that he had, if possible, to raise the money necessary to permit a proposal of marriage to Miss Andrews. He thus wrote to the only near relative who might provide him with the required income, his uncle William Suckling, a commissioner in the Customs Office. It was a letter revealing for the first time a certain ruthlessness, which underlay the affection he usually expressed to members of his family:

> My dear Uncle, there arrives in general a time in a man's life (who has friends), that either they place him in life in a situation that makes his application for anything further totally unnecessary, or give him help in a pecuniary way, if they can afford, and he deserves it ... The critical moment of my life is now arrived, that either I am to be happy or miserable: it depends solely on you. You may possibly think I am going to ask too much. I have led myself up with hopes you will not – till this trying moment. There is a lady I have seen, of a good family and connexions, but with a small fortune – £1000 I understand. The whole of my income does not exceed £130 per annum. Now I must come to the point: will you, if I should marry, allow me yearly £100 until my income is increased to that sum, either by employment or any other way? A very few years I hope would turn something up, if my friends will but exert themselves. If you will not give me the above sum, will you exert yourself with either Lord North [the Prime Minister] or Mr Jenkinson [the Secretary at War] to get me a guard-ship, or some employment in a public office where the attendance of the principle [sic] is not necessary...

RIGHT: *Viscount Hood, a mezzotint after a painting by Reynolds. Hood was Nelson's senior by 34 years, and at the time of their meeting in London an admiral. Nelson was later to say that he was 'the greatest sea officer I ever knew'.*

Nelson returned to London, to settle 'little matters' in his accounts and his uncle agreed to help him. But Nelson was informed that Miss Andrews was not ready for marriage. For distraction, he threw himself into 'running at the ring of pleasure'. He visited Lord Howe, First Lord of the Admiralty, and told him of his wish for a ship. He also dined with Lord Hood, 'who expressed the greatest friendship'. He thought of returning to the Continent, writing, 'I return to many charming women but no charming women will return with me.' Instead he visited Burnham Thorpe and Bath, until, in mid-March he received a new appointment, to the *Boreas*.

CHAPTER THREE

THE CARIBBEAN

ABOVE: *Wedgwood medallion of Lord Howe. As First Lord of the Admiralty in 1784, Howe gave Nelson command of the* Boreas.

B Y WHAT INTEREST HAD NELSON obtained his appointment to the 28-gun frigate, the *Boreas*, his brother William wished to know; to which Nelson replied that his recommendation to Lord Howe, First Lord of the Admiralty, was to have 'served with credit'. 'Anything in reason that I can ask', he continued in a somewhat pompous, self-righteous manner, 'I am sure of obtaining from his justice.'

Yet he was not too proud to expose his failures to Locker:

Since I have parted from you I have encountered many disagreeable adventures. The day after I left you, we sailed at daylight, just after high water. The d...d pilot – it makes me swear to think of it – ran the ship aground, where she lay with so little water that the people could walk round her till next high water. That night and part of the next day we lay below the Nore with a hard gale of wind and snow; Tuesday I got into the Downs [off Deal in Kent]; on Wednesday I got into a quarrel with a Dutch [East] Indiaman who had Englishmen on board, which we settled with some difficulty. The Dutchman has made a complaint against me; but the Admiralty fortunately have approved my conduct in the business, a thing they are not very guilty of where there is a likelihood of a scrape.

And, he continued:

Yesterday, to complete me, I was riding a blackguard horse that ran away with me at Common, carried me round all the works into Portsmouth, by the London gates, through the town, out at the gate that leads to Common, where there was a waggon in the road – which is very narrow that a horse could

RIGHT: *Dry Harbour in the Parish of St Ann, Jamaica. In trying to enforce the Navigation Acts and prevent illicit American trade with the West Indies, Nelson made himself extremely unpopular with the islanders, whom he considered 'as great rebels as ever were in America'.*

ABOVE: *Studies of a warship preparing to sail, going about and lying to, illustrated in* Liber Nauticus, *an instruction book for artists by Dominic and John Thomas Serres, 1805.*

barely pass. To save my legs, and perhaps my life, I was obliged to throw myself from the horse, which I did with great agility: but unluckily upon hard stones, which has hurt my back and my leg, but done no other mischief. It was a thousand to one that I had not been killed. To crown all, a young girl was riding with me; her horse ran away with mine; but most fortunately a gallant young man seized her horse's bridle a moment before I dismounted, and saved her from the destruction which she could not have avoided.

From Portsmouth the *Boreas* was to carry passengers out to the West Indies, including Lady Hughes, wife of the commander-in-chief of the station, and their daughter Rosy. Galled by the crowding of his ship, Nelson listed 34 people walking the quarter-deck at seven o'clock in the evening of 30 May 1784. They included George Andrews, brother of the young woman who had just demurred from his thoughts of marriage, and his own brother, William, who wanted to try the life of a naval chaplain. On arrival in the Leeward Islands, he was glad to part with the Hugheses: 'pleasant good people' but 'an incredible expense' on account of the cost to himself of their hospitality. From Jamaica, he wrote to Locker:

Collingwood is at Grenada, which is a great loss to me, for there is nobody that I can make a confidant of ... Was it not for Mrs Moutray, who is very, very good to me, I should almost hang myself at this infernal hole. Our Admiral [Hughes] is tolerable, but I do not like him; he bows and scrapes too much for me; his wife has an eternal clack, so that I go near them as little as possible. In short, I detest this country, but as I am embarked upon this station I shall remain in my ship.

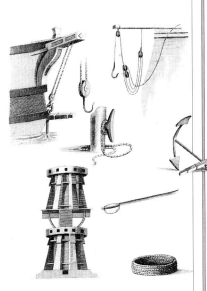

ABOVE: *Nautical details, including a capstan, anchor and cleat, from* Liber Nauticus.

LEFT: Boreas *off the Dutch island of St Eustatius in the Leeward Islands. Nelson commanded the 28-gun frigate* Boreas *from 1784 to 1787. He wrote to Locker from the ship, on hearing that there was a possibility of war in the East, that he was well prepared for action, 'well officered and manned'.*

Mrs Moutray was the wife of the commissioner of Antigua dockyard. Nelson first met her in July 1784 and he never passed English Harbour, Antigua, without calling at Windsor, the Moutrays' house. A loyal, loving wife, Mary Moutray was 26 years younger than her husband and only 32 in 1784. Evidently she found her friendships with visiting captains a relief from the tedium of island life. Collingwood had known her for longer than Nelson and achieved greater intimacy, including 'frizzing' her hair before a ball.

Mary made fun for them, at one time persuading the two men to draw one another's portraits, and naturally Nelson became attached to her. In February 1785, when he heard that his 'dear, sweet friend' was going back to England with her husband, he told his brother, 'I am really an April day: happy on her account, but truly grieved were I only to consider myself. Her equal I never saw in any country or in any situation.'

This country appears now intolerable, my dear friend being absent. It is barren indeed; not all the Rosys can give a spark of joy to me. English Harbour I hate the sight of and Windsor I detest. I once went up the hill to look at the spot where I spent more happy days than in any one spot in the world. E'en the trees drooped their heads, and the tamarind tree died; all was melancholy; the road is covered with thistles; let them grow; I shall never pull one of them up. By this time I hope she is safe in Old England. Heaven's choicest blessing go with her.

Nelson and Collingwood were to correspond with Mary for the rest of their lives. Her departure was partly due to her husband's ill health and partly as the result of a quarrel Nelson had had with him. As an old post-captain, he maintained his seniority over Nelson, even though, as dockyard commissioner, he had accepted a civil appointment.

Nelson's ill feeling for his island station was exacerbated by the islanders' determination to continue their now technically illegal trade with the merchants of the newly independent United States of America.

ABOVE: *Engraving after a drawing of Nelson by his friend Cuthbert Collingwood. Mary Moutray encouraged the two young officers to make portraits of each other.*

The Americans, when colonists, possessed almost all the trade from America to our West India islands; and on the return of peace, they forgot on this occasion that they became foreigners, and of course had no right to trade in the British colonies. Our governors and custom-house officers pretended that, by the Navigation Act, they had a right to trade, and all the West Indians wished what was so much for their interest.

Because they observed but did not attempt to stop the American trade, Nelson held Admiral Hughes and the officials with whom he conferred in the greatest contempt: 'the Admiral and all about him are great ninnies'. He wrote to Locker in January 1785:

The longer I am upon this station the worse I like it. Our Commander has not that opinion of his own sense that he ought to have. He is led by the advice of the islanders to admit the Yankees to a trade; at least to wink at it. He does not give himself that weight that I think an English Admiral ought to do. I, for one, am determined not to suffer the Yankees to come where my ship is ... After what I have said, you will believe I am not very popular with the people. They have never visited me, and I have not had a foot in any house since I have been on the station, and all for doing my duty by being *true to the interests of Great Britain* ... I am determined to suppress the admission of foreigners all in my power. I have told the Customs that I will complain if they admit any foreigner to any entry: an American arrives, sprung a leak, a mast, and what not, makes a protest, gets admittance, sells his cargo for ready money, goes to Martinico, buys molasses, and so round and round. But I hate them all.

Convinced that 'the residents of these islands are Americans by connexion and interest', and 'as great rebels as ever were in America, had they the power to show it', Nelson proceeded to seize American vessels he suspected of trading into British islands, 'which brought all parties upon me'.

ABOVE: *English Harbour, Antigua, from Great George Fort. 'This station is far from a pleasant one. The Admiral and all about him are great ninnies', Nelson wrote. Mary Moutray was married to the Commissioner of the naval dockyard at English Harbour.*

I was persecuted from one island to another, so that I could not leave my ship. But conscious rectitude bore me through it, and I was supported, when the business came to be understood, from home; and I proved (and an Act of Parliament has since established it) that a captain of a man-of-war is in duty bound to support all the maritime laws, by his Admiralty commission alone, without becoming a custom-house officer.

The one island where Nelson did go ashore was Nevis, where the island's president, John Herbert, hospitably entertained visiting captains in

ABOVE: *Engraving from Nelson's silhouette of Collingwood. Both portraits were presented to Mary Moutray in 1785 by her admirers.*

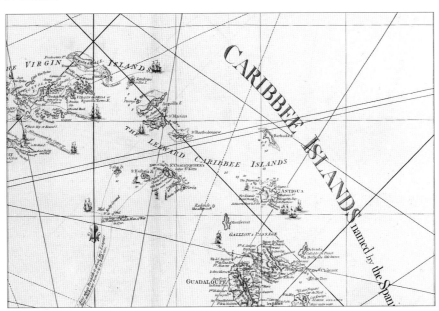

LEFT: *Map of the 'Caribbee Islands' published by Thomas Jefferys, Geographer to George III, in 1775. On it are shown Antigua, St Eustatius, St Kitts and Nevis, and the French island of Guadeloupe.*

Montpelier, a large house with verandas at the heart of a rich sugar plantation. But it was not until his third visit that he met Frances Nisbet, Herbert's niece. At 27, she was already widowed and had an infant son named Josiah. After a visit when Fanny, as she was known, had been absent, a friend reported to her:

> We have at last seen the little captain of the *Boreas*, of whom so much has been said. He came up just before dinner, much heated and was very silent yet seemed, according to the old adage, to think the more. He declined drinking any wine: but after dinner, when the president, as usual, has the three following toasts, the King, the Queen and the Royal Family, and Lord Hood, this strange man regularly filled his glass and observed that those were always bumper toasts with him; which, having drank, he uniformly passed the bottle and relapsed into his former taciturnity ... It was impossible for any of us to make out his real character; there was such

a reserve and sternness in his behaviour, with occasional sallies, though very transient, of a superior mind. Being placed by him, I endeavoured to rouse his attention by showing him all the civilities in my power: but I drew out little more than yes and no. If you, Fanny, had been there, we think you would have made something of him; for you have been in the habit of attending to these odd sort of people.

Nelson was less reserved with Josiah, with whom Herbert discovered him on his third visit to the island: 'Great God! If I did not find that great little man, of whom everybody is so afraid, playing in the next room under the dining table with Mrs Nisbet's child.' Perhaps through their common pleasure in playing with Josiah on his visits between May and August 1785, Nelson and Fanny Nisbet seemed to get on well. Fanny's manners reminded Nelson of Mary Moutray, while her 'mental accomplishments' seemed 'superior to most people of either sex'. By mid-August he was thinking of marriage. He proposed and she accepted. But the match was conditional upon adequate finance. Forced away by his duties, he left a letter for Herbert at Nevis suggesting as much, and wrote to Fanny:

> My dear Mrs Nisbit [sic], to say how anxious I have been, and am, to receive a line from Mr Herbert would be far beyond the descriptive powers of my pen. Most fervently do I hope his answer will be of such a tendency as to convey real pleasure, not only to myself, but also to you. For most sincerely do I love you, and I think that my affection is not only founded upon the principles of reason but also upon the basis of mutual attachment. Indeed, my charming Fanny, did [I] possess a million, my greatest pride and pleasure would be to share it with you; and as to living in a cottage with you, I should esteem it superior to living in a palace with any other I have yet met with. My age is enough to make me seriously reflect upon what I have offered, and commonsense tells me what a good choice I have made. The more I weigh you in my mind, the more reason I find to admire both your head and heart ... Don't think me rude by this entering into a correspondence with you.

LEFT: *Detail of a map from Jefferys's atlas or 'General Description of the West Indies taken from actual surveys and observations', showing the island of Nevis and part of nearby St Kitts.*

ABOVE: *Lithographic view of the mountainous island of Nevis with Charles Town, the capital of the island, in the foreground. Nevis was the one island where Nelson was made welcome ashore, particularly by the island's president, John Herbert.*

Herbert acknowledged the letter but, owing to the death of her aunt, Fanny did not reply. Fearing his letters might be 'troublesome', Nelson tried to explain the depth of his affection for her:

My greatest wish is to be united to you; and the foundation of all conjugal happiness, real love and esteem, is, I trust, what you believe I possess in the strongest degree towards you. I think Mr Herbert loves you too well not to let you marry the man of your choice, although he may not be so rich as others, provided his character and situation in life render such an union eligible. I declare solemnly that, did I not conceive I had the full possession of your heart, no consideration should make me accept your hand. We know that riches do not always insure happiness; and the world is convinced that I am superior to pecuniary considerations in my public and private life; as in both instances I might have been rich. But I will have done, leaving all my present feelings to operate in your breast; only of this truth be convinced, that I am, your affectionate, Horatio Nelson.

As Nelson made clear, pecuniary matters played upon his mind. To Collingwood he admitted that he wanted prize-money. Herbert would only offer distant help. He was unwilling to spare Fanny as his social hostess until he left Nevis in 1787, and even then, in the event of her marriage, would probably only allow her £200 or £300 a year. Nevertheless, when he died, Herbert would leave £20,000 and, if his daughter and heir also died, Fanny would have the major part of his property. As before, Nelson turned to his uncle, William Suckling:

> I open a business which perhaps you will smile at ... and say 'This Horatio is for ever in love' ... My present attachment is of pretty long standing ... My future happiness, I give you my honour, is now in your power; if you cannot afford to give me any thing for ever, you will, I am sure, trust to me that if ever I can afford it, I will return it to some part of your family ... if you will either give me, I will call it – I think you will do it – either one hundred a year for a few years, or a thousand pounds, how happy you will make a couple who will pray for you for ever. Don't disappoint me or my heart will break; trust to my honour to do a good turn for some other person if it is in my power. I can say no more but trust implicitly to your goodness, and pray let me know of your generous action by the first Packet.

Once again Suckling agreed to make Nelson an allowance.

Between his visits to Nevis, Nelson and Fanny maintained a happy, chatty correspondence throughout 1786. Nelson was even able to acknowledge to Fanny his feelings for Mary Moutray: 'I can't express what I feel for her and your good heart I am sure will sympathise with mine.' Their letters suggest that their affections for one another deepened and matured. In August he wrote:

> To write letters to you is the next greatest pleasure I feel to receiving them from you. What I experience when I read such as I am sure are the pure sentiments of your heart, my poor pen cannot express, nor indeed would I give much for any pen or head that could describe feelings of that kind: they are worth but little when that can happen.

BELOW: *Mary Moutray, a portrait drawing by John Downman. Nelson and Collingwood were desolated when she left for England. 'I took leave of her with a heavy heart,' Nelson wrote. 'What a treasure of a woman. God bless her.'*

NELSON'S SEAMEN

THE SEAMEN OF THE lower deck were distinctive in dress and language. Their faces showed the effects of sun, rain, wind and sea, their hands were hardened and tarred from hauling on ropes and reefing sails, and they possessed a carefree indifference to hardship, danger or death. On shore their revelling was notorious. At sea their energy and morale shaped the spirit of a ship.

At the outbreak of war the Admiralty resorted to impressment to increase the number of ships it could man. Trained seamen were taken from merchant ships or sought out by press gangs on shore. In this way, as well as by voluntary recruitment, especially of foreigners, the size of the Navy was increased from 17,000 men in 1792 to 143,000 men in 1808. In 1795 two Quota Acts were passed requiring counties and towns to supply a prescribed number of men to the Navy. These men were landmen, not trained seamen, who served as the labourers on board. Magistrates took advantage of the quotas to remove local undesirables.

Punishments were generally inflicted with the cat-o'-nine-tails, and floggings took place at least once a week. Like the bench of magistrates on shore, the captain had the power to impose summary punishments, of up to a dozen lashes, without sending men to trial by court-martial. Indeed this was sometimes regarded as preferable to court-martial, where 17 offences, including desertion, were

LEFT: *Drawing of a scene on the gun deck of a man-of-war in harbour in about 1800. Sailors disport themselves with women who have been rowed out to them in 'bumboats'.*

punishable by the death penalty. But captains could, and sometimes did, inflict more than their regulation dozen for neglect of duty, disobedience or contempt.

Seamen who avoided the eye and rope's end of the boatswain's mate for the most part had a relatively good life. Their diet was varied by regulation and was better than many would have received on shore. They had their accumulated 'grog' allowances on occasions for celebration, and in port 'bumboats' brought women out to each ship as she arrived.

Discontent manifested itself when seamen thought themselves subject to injustice. The Spithead and Nore mutinies in 1797 arose from a collection of grievances: low wage rates, which had not been raised for a century, the poor quality and short measure of provisions, the lack of shore leave, and limitations in the care of the sick and pay of the wounded. There were in addition complaints about the brutality of some officers. The mutinies succeeded to the extent that pay was improved, short measure in the supply of provisions was prohibited, and the most brutal officers were removed, but 412 leaders of the Nore mutiny were tried, of which 29 were hanged, 29 were imprisoned and 9 were flogged.

Nelson was loved by his seamen because he shared many of their hardships, appealed to their affections and manifestly took an interest in their welfare. In 1804 he wrote himself to the Admiralty to complain of the poor quality of the 'frocks and trousers'.

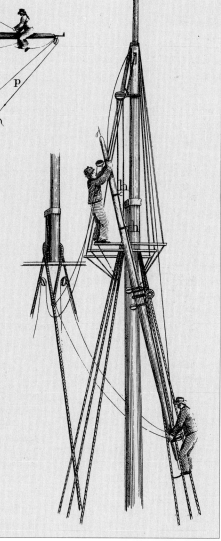

ABOVE: *'Bending the foresail', with men up on the yard.*

RIGHT: *'Getting top-gallant yards across braces', with a man up on the cross-trees. Both illustrations of naval practice are from Darcy Lever's* Young Sea-Officer's Sheet Anchor, *1808.*

My heart yearns to you – it is with you; my mind dwells upon nought else but you. Absent from you, I feel no pleasure; it is you, my dearest Fanny, who are everything to me. Without you, I care not for this world, for I have found lately nothing in it but vexation and trouble. These, you are well convinced, are my present sentiments; God almighty grant they may never change. Nor do I think they will: indeed, there is, as far as human knowledge can judge, a moral certainty they cannot; for it must be real affection that brings us together, not interest or compulsion, which make so many unhappy.

As always, however, his commitment to her was qualified by his devotion to duty: 'Our country has the first demand for our services, and private convenience, or happiness, must ever give way to the Public good.' It was a qualification that had hardened once he had been given local command in the West Indies. In the same letter he wrote:

ABOVE: *British life in the West Indies: ladies being offered and enticed to buy wares by linen traders in a market.*

> As you begin to know sailors, have you not often heard that salt water and absence always wash away love? Now, I am such a heretic as not to believe that faith; for behold, every morning since my arrival, I have had six pails of salt water at daylight poured upon my head, and instead of finding what seamen say to be true, I perceive the contrary effect; and if it goes on so contrary to the prescription you must see me before my fixed time. At first I bore absence tolerably, but now it is almost insupportable; and by-and-by I expect it will be quite so. But patience is a virtue; and I must exercise it upon this occasion, whatever it costs my feelings.

ABOVE: *Frances Nisbet by Daniel Orme, 1798. 'We shall come together as two persons most sincerely attached to each other from friendship,' Nelson wrote.*

In December 1786 Prince William returned to the West Indies in command of the frigate *Pegasus* and was placed under Nelson's command. The social festivities laid on for the Prince wearied Nelson. They were another duty to

ABOVE: *Nelson described the West Indies as 'the* grand theatre *of actions'. Here, Admiral Barrington's squadron lands troops to seize the island of St Lucia from the French, in 1778.*

attend to and kept him longer from Fanny, for he could not 'with propriety' leave His Royal Highness by himself.

The Prince interested himself in Nelson's private life and enjoyed teasing him. Nelson wrote to Fanny:

> His Royal Highness often tells me he believes I am married, for he never saw a lover so easy or say so little of the object he has a regard for. When I tell him I certainly am not, he says, 'Then he is sure I must have a great esteem for you and that it is not what is (vulgarly) – I do not much like the use of that word – called love'. He is right: my love is founded on esteem, the only foundation that can make the passion last.

It was Prince William who fixed the date of the wedding. He promised to be there to give the bride away, and in March 1787 a change of plans permitted him to go to Nevis with Nelson. He insisted that 'it is hardly probable he should see me there again ... and should be much mortified if impediments were thrown in the way' of their marriage. Nelson and Fanny thus were married at Montpelier five days later, on 11 March 1787.

Prince William was to serve under Nelson until May 1787. Nelson's deference to him amounted almost to sycophancy – 'as an individual I love him; as a Prince I honour and revere him'. He allowed this respect for the royal person to interfere with his judgement on professional matters involving the Prince, which were referred to the Board of Admiralty.

In June 1787 Nelson returned to England. Fanny went with her uncle on a West Indiaman, but the *Boreas* was delayed from paying off until November of that year, so that Nelson and his new wife did not really settle down to life in England until 1788. On half pay and without a home, they moved into the parsonage house at Burnham Thorpe with Edmund Nelson. Edmund had 30 acres of church land to till and, as much to occupy himself as to grow crops, Nelson turned farmer.

It was not an easy or a particularly happy time. Nelson failed to gain for Fanny a place in the household establishment of Prince William, and Fanny felt the winter cold. Edmund was conscious of the crowding and, after a while, moved to a small cottage at nearby Burnham Ulph. Nelson felt neglected by the Admiralty when he failed to receive a commission to another ship and, on receiving negative or no replies to his applications, gave way to melancholy or to a 'tempest of passions'. Furthermore, when hostilities with Spain seemed likely in 1790 and he visited Lord Hood, now an Admiralty Commissioner, he was mortified by Hood's speech, 'never to be effaced from my memory, viz: that the King was impressed with an unfavourable opinion of me'.

This may have been due to his friendship with Prince William, or to the hornet's nest he had stirred up in the West Indian merchant community. A writ

ABOVE: *'Board Room at the Admiralty' from the* Microcosm of London *by Thomas Rowlandson and A. C. Pugin. Charts are rolled up above the fireplace, and at the back of the room is the circular dial of a wind indicator.*

for damages on behalf of two American captains whose ships Nelson had seized was actually served on Fanny at Burnham Thorpe when Nelson was away. Alternatively, it may have been due to the administrative misjudgements that were referred to the Admiralty shortly before he left the West Indies.

After the revolution in France in 1789, and with the growth of reforming societies in Britain, Nelson began to take an interest in the economic state of agricultural labourers. And as he – and the political situation of the country – grew more desperate, he revived his correspondence with Prince William:

> Your Royal Highness will not, I trust, deem it improper (although I have no doubt it will be thought unnecessary) at this time to renew my expressions of invariable attachment not only to your Royal Highness but to my King: for I think very soon every individual will be called forth to show himself, if I may judge from this county, where societies are formed and forming on principles certainly inimical to our present constitution both in Church and State, of which our dissenters are the head, and in this county they have great riches ... In what way it might be in the power of such an humble individual as myself to best serve my King has been matter of serious consideration, and no way appeared to me so proper as asking for a ship; and on Saturday last Lord Chatham [First Lord of the Admiralty] received my letter asking for the command of one; but as I have hitherto been disappointed in all my applications to his Lordship, I can hardly expect any answer to my letter, which has always been the way I have been treated: but neither at sea, nor on shore, through the caprice of a Minister, can my attachment to my King be shaken; and which will never end but with my life.

It was only with the outbreak of the Revolutionary war with France in 1793 that he was eventually to gain the summons to the Admiralty for which he had waited so long.

LEFT: *Admiralty House from Whitehall. Nelson wrote to the Earl of Chatham at the Admiralty, 'I am sensible I have no great interest to recommend me, nor have I had conspicuous opportunities of distinguishing myself: but thus far ... I can say that no opportunity has passed by; and that I have ever been a zealous officer.'*

THE QUEST FOR GLORY

ABOVE: *Head, quarter and stern of a 74-gun ship, three details from* Liber Nauticus *by Dominic Serres and his son John Thomas. They were leading marine artists noted for their accurate draughtsmanship.*

N ELSON'S VISIT TO THE ADMIRALTY took place early in January 1793, and on the seventh of the month, before taking formal command of his ship, he wrote happily to Fanny:

Post nubila Phoebus: – After clouds comes sunshine. The Admiralty so smile upon me that really I am as much surprised as when they frowned. Lord Chatham yesterday made many apologies for not having given me a ship before this time, and said that, if I chose to take a sixty-four to begin with, I should be appointed to one as soon as she was ready; and whenever it was in his power, I should be removed into a seventy-four. Everything indicates war. One of our ships looking into Brest has been fired into; the shot is now at the Admiralty. You will send my father this news, which I am sure will please him. Love to Josiah, and believe me, Your most affectionate, Horatio Nelson.

The result was, as he later recounted,

On 30 January 1793, I was commissioned in the very handsomest way for the *Agamemnon*, 64; and was put under the command of that great man and excellent officer, Lord Hood, appointed to the command in the Mediterranean.

The appointment marked the beginning of a return to favour that four years later was to culminate in distinction at the Battle of Cape St Vincent.

His letters to Fanny during this period record his increasing confidence and ambition. But while Nelson rejoiced at his return to life at sea, Fanny was miserable at being left, especially as Nelson took her son Josiah with him, and she fretted at the dangers to which both might be subject.

RIGHT: *Nicholas Pocock's watercolour of the* Agamemnon *in 1795. Two years earlier Nelson had written from the* Agamemnon, *'have no doubt but we shall acquit ourselves well, should the French give us a meeting.'*

Although full of news and ending affectionately, Nelson's letters reveal that to him their relationship was becoming one of mere practical necessity. He became irritated with Fanny's inefficiencies and from Chatham, once the *Agamemnon* was fitted, he scolded:

> You forgot to send my things ... by the Sheerness boat ... I have got a keg of tongues which I suppose you ordered, and also a trunk from Wells, Norfolk, and a hamper of three hams, and a breast of bacon, and a face, not very well packed, there being no straw between them and the motion of the waggon has rubbed them very much. However they will do.

From the English Channel the *Agamemnon* accompanied Lord Hood to Toulon. From there, in August, Nelson was sent to Naples with an appeal to the King, Ferdinand IV, to send troops to Toulon to help the allies – Britain, Spain, Sardinia and the French royalists – to hold the French naval base against a besieging French republican army. On his arrival in Naples on 10 September Vesuvius was in eruption, 'the lava spreading from the top and rolling down the mountain in great streaks of fire'.

Nelson delivered his despatches to Sir William Hamilton, the British Envoy, and at the embassy, met Sir William's wife, Emma. She was, he reported to Fanny, 'a young woman of amiable manners' who did 'honour to the station to which she was raised'. He took Josiah on shore with other midshipmen, where Emma was 'wonderfully kind and good to him'. He also met the King, nick-named '*il Re Nasone*' after his large ill-shaped nose, and the Queen, Maria Carolina, whom the Neapolitans called '*Polpett Mbocca*', 'Mouthful of Rissole', after the way she gabbled her words. Through Sir John Acton, the expatriate Englishman who had become principal minister at the Court, Sir William and Nelson secured the promise of 6,000 Neapolitan troops for the siege of Toulon. This success crowned an immediate liking that Nelson had formed for Sir William: 'You are a man after my own heart ... you do business in my own way.'

From Toulon Nelson was despatched to Tunis, to assist in putting pressure on the Bey to hand over to the British a French convoy of Levant merchantmen;

ABOVE: *Sir William Hamilton, British Envoy to the Neapolitan court. He was a classical scholar, connoisseur and archaeologist as well as diplomat. Print after a portrait painted in Naples in 1794 by Hugh Douglas Hamilton.*

then to command a squadron of smaller vessels off the coast of Italy, to protect British trade into the Gulf of Genoa while seizing enemy ships. In December the French republican army, which included Napoleon Bonaparte with the artillery, took control of Toulon harbour, forcing the British to burn much of the French fleet and to seek a new Mediterranean base for their own.

Hood deputed Nelson to begin blockading the French-occupied island of Corsica, where the chief partisan leader, General Paoli, was willing to work with the British to eject the French. Following occupation of the port of San Fiorenzo by British troops, the fortresses at Bastia and Calvi had to be reduced. Nelson repeatedly urged that Hood should take the former by landing seamen, marines and soldiers, a landing in which he, with his local knowledge, would take the leading naval part. When the army commander, General Dundas, opposed committing troops, Nelson still volunteered to lead the seamen, arguing that not to make an attack would be a 'national disgrace'.

He discovered that the French garrison comprised at least three times the force the British could assemble but kept the information to himself. 'What would the immortal Wolfe have done? As he did, beat the enemy, if he perished in the attempt.' Eventually, Nelson was given command of the landings and the construction of the batteries and, after a five-week siege in May 1794, Bastia surrendered. The capitulation was principally due to hunger rather than the bombardment, but Nelson was mortified when the public report of the capture failed to give him the credit he thought was his.

The siege of Bastia was quickly followed by that of Calvi. Here bombardment by batteries seemed to present the only means of reducing the town, and Nelson was again given responsibility for getting the guns in place. The landing in a narrow, rocky inlet, followed by haulage over more than two miles across rough, boulder-strewn terrain, much of it uphill, presented numerous challenges. It took two weeks to begin building the emplacements. This, and then sighting the guns, was dangerous work, because the batteries were within reach of the enemy guns on the walls of the town; casualties were common. One day three guns were damaged or destroyed; and on 12 July Nelson himself was

ABOVE: *French popular print of Napoleon at the siege of Toulon in 1793. Napoleon is depicted on the right, helping to load a republican gun after the rammer, lying at his feet, had been killed by royalist fire.*

ABOVE: *Map of the harbour at Toulon showing the fortifications and the disposition of forces during the siege. Napoleon's success at Toulon led to his appointment to command the French campaign in Italy.*

wounded. Shot, landing on the rampart, threw up sand and stones. Cut and bruised about the face, there was much blood but little apparent harm. He did not mention the damage to his eye to his wife until 4 August, and only described the consequences for his vision four days later:

> I most fortunately escaped by only having my right eye nearly deprived of its sight. It was cut down, but as far recovered as to be able to distinguish light from darkness, but as to all the purpose of its use, it is gone. However the blemish is nothing, not to be perceived unless told.

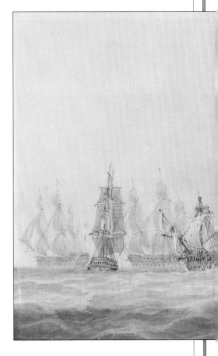

But recovery was slow, with relapses. By the end of January he was writing, 'my eye is grown worse, and is in almost total darkness, and very painful at times', though adding bravely, 'but never mind, I can see very well with the other'.

On 10 August 1794, short of ammunition, the French surrendered. Again, though he thought his part vital, Nelson felt he was not given the credit he deserved when the report on the siege was published in the *London Gazette.* 'My diligence is not mentioned', he wrote to Suckling:

> Others, for keeping succours out of Calvi for a few summer months are handsomely mentioned. *Such things are.* I have got upon a subject near to my heart, which is full when I think of the treatment I have received: every man who had any considerable share in the reduction has got some place or other. I, only I, am without reward. The taking of Corsica, like the taking of St Juan's [in 1780] has cost me money. St Juan's cost near £500 [in expenses and loss of pay through illness]; Corsica has cost me £300, an eye, and a cut across my back; and my money, I find, cannot be repaid me. Nothing but my anxious endeavours to serve my country makes me bear up against it; but I sometimes am ready to give all up.

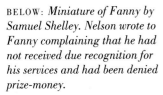

BELOW: *Miniature of Fanny by Samuel Shelley. Nelson wrote to Fanny complaining that he had not received due recognition for his services and had been denied prize-money.*

Grievance that his services were going unnoticed became a theme in Nelson's letters to his wife. His despondency grew when Hood, who seemed to favour him, went home and was replaced by Admiral Hotham. Nevertheless he enjoyed good health and grew 'quite stout'.

ABOVE: *The capture of the* Ça Ira *in the Gulf of Genoa on 14 March 1795. The day before, Nelson described the French ship as 'a perfect wreck, her sails hanging in tatters, mizzen topmast and cross-jack yards shot away'.*

That winter the *Agamemnon* repaired to Leghorn, a convenient refuge from the winter storms for the British fleet while it blockaded Toulon. There Nelson found solace in the company of an opera singer, Adelaide Correglia. On his departure a note appealed to her to 'think of him always'. On visits to Leghorn Nelson repeatedly entertained her, to the embarrassment of some of his friends. In summer 1795 Captain Fremantle reported disapprovingly, 'dined with Nelson. Dolly aboard ... he makes himself ridiculous with that woman.'

Nelson continued to write to Fanny with affection and to impart to her his ambitions. Her letters to him were full of anxiety: she was 'continually in a hurry and fret about him'. Her timidity was a foil to his bravado. On 10 March 1795, when the French fleet of 15 ships of the line was discovered out of port and chased by the British, he explained to her the fatalism that had to come to rule his life:

> Whatever may be my fate, I have no doubt in my own mind but that my conduct will be such as will not bring a blush on the face of my friends: the lives of all are in the hands of Him who knows best whether to preserve mine or not; to his will do I resign myself. My character and good name are in my keeping. Life with disgrace is dreadful. A glorious death is to be envied; and if anything happens to me, recollect that death is a debt we must all pay, and whether now, or in a few years, can be but of little consequence.

The chase of the French achieved only a skirmish. But it marked the beginning of Nelson's 'reputation' as one who was prepared to risk death. Two of the French vessels collided and the *Ça Ira*, an 80-gun ship, fell astern. Nelson got up close behind the damaged ship, tacking from side to side and firing broadsides through her stern windows. The *Ça Ira* was unable to return fire and was reduced to a wreck. However, after the French fleet had turned to join battle, Hotham recalled the *Agamemnon*. Next day the *Ça Ira* and the *Censeur*, which had her in tow, were both cut off and taken by the British. Nelson discovered that the former had about 350 killed or wounded, mainly from his bombardment. Excited by his part in the action, he fumed at Hotham's caution, writing to Fanny:

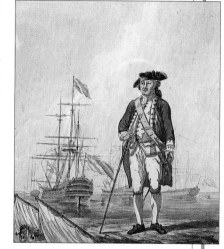

ABOVE: *Dress of an admiral, the rank to which Nelson now aspired. In this 1777 print by Dominic Serres, the admiral wears the sash and star of the Order of the Bath. Nelson was to be created a knight of the order in 1797.*

I wish to be an Admiral and in command of the English fleet. I should very soon either do much or be ruined. My disposition cannot bear tame and slow measures. Sure I am, had I commanded our fleet on the 14th, that either the whole French fleet would have graced my triumph, or I should have been in a confounded scrape. I went on board [Admiral] Hotham so soon as our firing grew slack in the van, and the *Ça Ira* and *Censeur* struck, to propose to him leaving our two crippled ships, the two prizes, and four frigates, to themselves and to pursue the enemy, but he is much cooler than myself and said 'We must be contented. We have done very well', but had we taken 10 sail and allowed the 11th to have escaped if possible to have been got at, I could never call it well done. [Admiral] Goodall backed me. I got him to write to the Admiral, but it would not do. We should have had such a day as I believe the annals of England never produced ... I verily believe if the Admiral can get hold of them once more but we shall do better, and if he does but get us close, we will have the whole fleet. Nothing can stop the courage of English seamen.

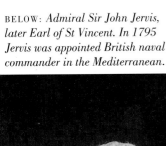

BELOW: *Admiral Sir John Jervis, later Earl of St Vincent. In 1795 Jervis was appointed British naval commander in the Mediterranean.*

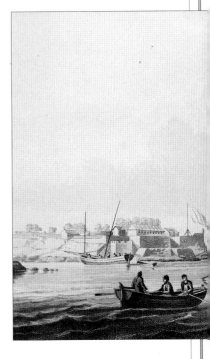

As a result of the action, he himself was already gaining a reputation for his bellicosity, and having verses written about him. He continued:

I am so covered with laurels that you will hardly find my little face. At one period I am 'the dear Nelson', 'the amiable Nelson', 'the fiery Nelson'. However nonsensical these things are, they are better than censure, and we are all subject and open to flattery.

The French navy was largely trapped in port and unpractised both in seamanship and battle. In early July 1795 there was another skirmish, 'but they being neither Seamen nor Officers, gave us many advantages'. His attitude recommended him to

Sir John Jervis, who replaced Hotham in November 1795, and his feeling of success was enhanced by Jervis treating him 'more like an associate than a subordinate officer'.

Stationed off Genoa, he was ordered to take and detain all outward-bound vessels sailing for France, to whatever nation they belonged. Politically it was a difficult position because he had to avoid giving offence to the Genoese, who remained neutral. At the same time, the small squadron he commanded patrolled the coast of the Gulf of Genoa, seizing French privateers that sheltered in ports along the coast and ventured out every night. Keeping in touch with the Austrian army on shore, it was a task he performed to the approval of Jervis, who in 1796 transferred him to a larger ship, the *Captain* of 74 guns. He appointed him commodore – a temporary rank for a captain, giving him specific authority over others – and also commended him to the First Lord of the Admiralty.

Such approval kept him from requesting leave to visit Fanny. As he explained to her in June 1796:

> if I am to serve, it is better I should serve in this country, where I am known and respected, than to take my chance of being sent home and ordered to another station.

ABOVE: Chasse-marée, *a French fishing boat of a similar rig to the faster, heavily manned ones used as coastal privateers. Nelson was charged with challenging such vessels in the Gulf of Genoa.*

He now realized that his reputation in England depended on the public notice he received. Knowing he had to beware of unhelpful connections, he observed to Fanny in August, 'I had a letter a few days past from the Duke of Clarence [as Prince William had become] assuring me of his unalterable friendship. Will this ever do good? I will however take care it shall do me no harm.' He was acutely conscious of the value of favourable mention in the *London Gazette*, in which the government selectively published its official correspondence relating to the conduct of the war. He particularly wanted his own reports published. He thus continued to Fanny:

Had all my actions been gazetted not one fortnight would have passed. Let those enjoy their brag and one day or other I will have a large Gazette to myself. I feel that one day or other such an opportunity will be given me. I cannot, if I am in the field of glory, be kept out of sight ... Probably my services may be forgot (by the Great) by the time I get home but my mind will not forget nor fail to feel a degree of consolation and of applause superior to undeserved rewards. Wherever there is anything to be done, there Providence is sure to direct my steps, and ever credit must be given me in spite of envy ...

With rising self-approval, he continued:

But even the French respect me: their Minister at Genoa on occasion of answering a note of mine returning wearing apparel says, 'Your nation, Sir, and mine is made to show all the people of the earth examples of generosity as well as valour.' I shall relate another anecdote, all vanity to myself, but you will partake of it. A person wrote me a letter and directed as follows, 'Horatio Nelson, Genoa'. On being asked how he could direct in such a manner his answer was ... 'Sir, there is but one H.N. in the world.' The letter certainly came directly. At Genoa, where I have stopped all their trade, I am beloved and respected by both Senate and lower order. If a man is fearful of his vessel being stopped, he comes and asks me; if I give him a paper or say all is right, they are content. I am known in Italy, not a kingdom or a state where my name will be forgot. This is *my* Gazette.

ABOVE: *'Master and Commander, with a sloop of war', an illustration by Dominic Serres.*

RIGHT: *The Battle of Cape St Vincent, 14 February 1797, with Nelson's ship the* Captain *astern of her two prizes, the* San Nicolas *and the* San Josef. *Afterwards, Nelson wrote to William Suckling, 'you will receive pleasure for the share I had in making it a most brilliant day, the most so of any day I know in the annals of England.'*

Fanny continued to press him to return home, Nelson replying that this depended on the course of the war:

You ask me when I shall come home. I believe, when an honourable peace is made or a Spanish war, which may draw our fleet out of the Mediterranean.

God knows I shall come to not a sixpence richer than when I set out, but I verily believe with a much better constitution. If I ever feel unwell, it is when I have no active employment, that is but seldom.

Spain changed sides in October 1796, to ally herself with France, and the balance of naval power in the western Mediterranean inevitably shifted in their favour. As Nelson had anticipated, the British fleet was withdrawn westward of the Straits of Gibraltar, and the British military forces likewise withdrew from territories recently hard won. Nelson was required first to evacuate the British garrison in Bastia, then to evacuate Elba. With his commodore's flag in the frigate *La Minerve*, which was commanded by Captain George Cockburn, and in the company of another frigate, the *Blanche*, he left Gibraltar for Elba early in December 1796.

Off Cartagena the two ships were attacked by two Spanish vessels of similar force. Although 45 of *La Minerve's* crew were killed or wounded, one of the Spanish frigates, the *Santa Sabina*, was taken, only to be lost again the next morning when a Spanish squadron approached. Lieutenant Thomas Masterman

BELOW: *Section of a first-rate ship, from Hervey's* Naval History. *The diagram shows the quarter deck, the upper deck and command position between the main and mizzen masts; the upper gun deck forward of the mainmast; the lower gun deck; the orlop deck and the hold.*

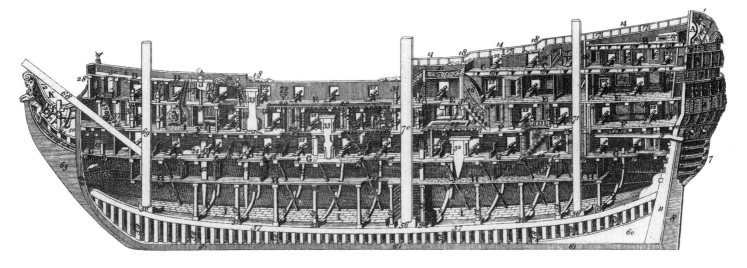

Hardy of *La Minerve* was commanding the prize crew on the *Santa Sabina* and they were captured when the frigate was given up. But, to Nelson's delight, his report to Jervis was printed in the *London Gazette*.

The success with which *La Minerve* fought owed a great deal to the training and management of the ship under Cockburn. Later, back in London, Nelson had a gold-hilted presentation sword made for Cockburn in recognition of the debt he owed him.

At Elba there was time to enjoy the Christmas ball before a small convoy was escorted to Gibraltar. There Nelson heard that the Spanish fleet had left Cartagena and had passed through the Straits of Gibraltar heading for Cadiz, which was being blockaded by Jervis.

Sailing westward through the Straits immediately, Nelson in *La Minerve* slipped through the shadows of the Spanish fleet that night, to reach Jervis in time to warn him of the approach of the enemy. Nelson himself then returned on board his own vessel, the 74-gun *Captain*, which took its place in the British line. On 14 February 1797, some miles off the Spanish Cape of St Vincent, Nelson had his first opportunity to distinguish himself in a line battle.

Jervis had only 15 ships of the line, to the Spanish 27, which were sailing in two divisions. Crossing courses on opposite tacks, the British fleet passed between the two halves of the Spanish fleet when Jervis ordered his ships to tack in succession in order to close with the Spaniards. Watching the Spanish manoeuvres, Nelson realized that unless British ships intervened more quickly, the two enemy divisions would close up, becoming stronger in their united force. Although without permission, and by his action weakening the British formation, Nelson precipitately turned the *Captain* out of line and thrust it into the gap between the two halves of the Spanish fleet.

ABOVE: *Key to the figures in Daniel Orme's painting of 'Lord St Vincent's Victory' on page 75. Nelson is at the centre right of the plate, with Captain Berry beside him and the Spanish captain beneath.*

SIR WILLIAM HAMILTON

IR WILLIAM HAMILTON was born in December 1730. Between 1747 and 1758 he served as an officer in the third regiment of the foot guards and was in Holland during the last year of the War of the Austrian Succession. In 1751, when the future King George III became Prince of Wales and immediate heir to the throne, Hamilton became his equerry. Two years later he was promoted to captain, and took part in the opening stages of the Seven Years' War against France. Soon afterwards he seems to have realized that his growing interests in the arts could only be satisfied by a more settled life than that of the professional soldier. His decision to resign his commission was probably also affected by his marriage in January 1758 to Catherine Barlow, through whom he obtained an estate near Swansea worth almost £5,000 a year. She died in 1782.

With the succession of the Prince of Wales to the throne in 1760, Hamilton was elected to the House of Commons for the pocket borough of Midhurst, in Sussex. At that time his wife was in delicate health, and this may have been a factor in inducing him in 1764 to take the post of Envoy Extraordinary and Minister Plenipotentiary to the kingdom of Naples and Sicily, later known as the Two Sicilies.

After Paris, Naples was then the largest city on the continent of Europe, where great wealth and luxury existed in close proximity to abject poverty and squalor. Hamilton and the young king, Ferdinand IV, established a friendly relationship that was to last for many years.

Charming, intellectual and energetic, Hamilton soon became known for his hospitality, his dancing at court and his outdoor pursuits. In four years he ascended Vesuvius 22 times. He employed an artist to record in sketches all stages of volcanic eruptions and by 1767 had formed a collection of volcanic earths and minerals which he presented to the British Museum. His studies of volcanoes were published between 1766 and 1780 in the *Philosophical Transactions of the Royal Society*, of which he was elected a Fellow in 1766.

At the same time Hamilton was collecting Greek and Roman vases, terracottas, glass, bronzes, ivories, coins, gems, gold, ornaments and other objects. He gradually formed his own museum and in 1766-7 had a four-volume illustrated catalogue printed. In 1772 he sold the collection to the British Museum for £8,400, a sum for which the trustees had to obtain a parliamentary grant – the purchase formed the foundation of the current collection of the Department of Greek and Roman Antiquities. Hamilton then renounced collecting.

Inevitably, however, the passion was revived. His new collection was thinned by occasional presentations to the British Museum and friends, to whom he also sold major items. His collection of vases gradually became finer than his previous one, and it grew so large that a five-volume catalogue was produced from 1791. When the French threatened Naples in 1798, he sent the collection for sale in England on board the British warship *Colossus*. To his great chagrin, the ship was wrecked off the Scilly Isles. Fortunately, however, 16 of his 24 cases of items were saved and sold for 4,500 guineas.

In 1784 Hamilton visited England and, at the house of his nephew Charles Greville, was introduced to Emma Hart. Greville persuaded him to invite Emma to visit him on his return to Naples, and she arrived with her mother, Mrs 'Cadogan', in April 1786. At the end of that year Emma became his mistress.

They were married in September 1791 while in England. It was two years later, after Emma had settled to life as Hamilton's wife, that Nelson visited them in Naples, briefly and for the first time.

RIGHT: *Sir William Hamilton in a portrait painted by David Allan which was given by the painter to the British Museum.*

ABOVE AND FAR LEFT: *Three plates from Sir William's book on volcanoes, Campi Phlegraei ('Fiery Fields'): the upper two show Vesuvius erupting on the night of 8 August 1779 and the following morning; the lower shows a view of the discovery of the Temple of Isis at Pompeii. They illustrate Sir William's interest in vulcanology and archaeology.*

The approaching Spanish vessels began to pile up all about him. Followed and supported by British ships, a pell-mell battle developed.

The *Captain* was soon reduced to a near wreck: she was without her foretop-mast, 'not a sail, shroud or rope left, her wheel shot away, and incapable of further service in the line or in chase'. However she was close to the Spanish *San Josef*, a first rate of 112 guns, and the *San Nicolas* of 80. Nelson had the *Captain* manoeuvred against the latter and, with rigging interlocking, called for boarders, whom he accompanied through the stern windows of the Spanish

LEFT: *Nelson leading the boarding party on to the* San Josef *from the deck of the* San Nicolas. *'"Nelson's patent bridge for boarding First-rates" will be a saying never forgotten in this fleet, where all do me the justice I deserve', wrote Nelson.*

vessel. They fought their way to the forecastle and the surviving Spanish officers surrendered. At that moment pistols and muskets began firing from the *San Josef* into the British boarders. Calling for reinforcements and for soldiers to return the fire, Nelson led his people into the large first rate. As before, the Spanish officers surrendered. Nelson, receiving their swords, gave them to William Fearney, one of his bargemen, 'who put them with the greatest sangfroid under his arm'.

It was the greatest moment of Nelson's life. As the British ships passed the captured Spanish vessels and the shattered *Captain*, each gave Nelson three cheers. Although he could have been court-martialled for falling out of the British line, he was received on the flagship by Jervis with gratitude. Wishing to publicize his actions, Nelson afterwards wrote an account of his part in the battle that was attested by two witnesses and sent to Captain Locker to be published in the newspapers. When news of the battle reached London, Jervis was created Earl of St Vincent, while Nelson was made a Knight of the Bath. His promotion to rear-admiral had, by coincidence, been published just before news of the victory had reached England.

RIGHT: One of several engravings published to commemorate the Battle of Cape St Vincent, 14 February 1797. Nelson's father wrote to him from Bath, 'joy sparkles in every eye and desponding Britain draws back her sabled veil and smiles'.

CHAPTER FIVE

VICTORY IN THE MEDITERRANEAN

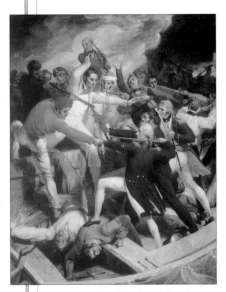

ABOVE: *Hand to hand fighting during the blockade of Cadiz, one of the notable episodes of Nelson's career painted by Richard Westall. 'The Spaniards fought like devils and seemed resolved to win from the Admiral the laurels of his former victory.'*

LEARNING OF THE PART Nelson had played in the battle off Cape St Vincent, Fanny wrote to him, 'I sincerely hope, my dear husband, that all these wonderful and desperate actions such as boarding ships you will leave to others. And she went on, 'With the protection of a Supreme Being you have acquired a character or name which all hands agree cannot be greater, therefore rest satisfied.'

'I shall come one day or other laughing back when we will retire from the busy scenes of life', he assured her, encouraging her in his absence to consider the purchase of a house for his return. He claimed he could afford little more than a cottage, even with a small public pension, but 'my chains, medals and ribbons with a contented mind are all sufficient'.

In truth, however, Nelson was still carried by his ambition. Boarding the *San Josef*, Nelson had been heard to shout, 'Westminster Abbey! or glorious victory!' – death or glory. By being prepared to make the greatest sacrifice, he had hit upon a means of achieving fame and public adulation. It entailed a readiness to take risks not only with his own life but with those of his seamen.

As events were to reveal, Nelson's preoccupation with the conclusion impaired his judgement concerning the method by which it was to be reached. Moreover, contrary to the wishes of his wife, it was necessary to commit his own person to physical danger more deliberately than ever before. This last he readily acknowledged:

In April [1797] I hoisted my flag as rear-admiral of the blue, and was sent to bring down the garrison of Porto Ferrajo [Elba]; which service performed, I shifted my flag from the *Captain* to the *Theseus* on 27 May, and was employed

RIGHT: *Nelson on the quarter deck of the* San Josef *receiving the sword of surrender from the Spanish captain, painted by Daniel Orme. Nelson wrote to the Mayor of Norwich, 'being born in the County of Norfolk, I beg leave to present the sword to the City of Norwich, in order to its being preserved as a memento of the event, and of my affection for my native county.'*

BELOW: *'John Bull offering Little Boney fair play', a cartoon by James Gillray of John Bull, dressed as a British tar, taunting Napoleon and challenging him to invade Britain.*

LEFT: *The blockade of Cadiz. Nelson, now promoted to Rear-Admiral of the Blue, issued the order to all captains of ships under his command, 'when you board any ship bound to Cadiz, to acquaint the master of such ship that the port is blockaded, and that he must seek another market.'*

in the command of the inner squadron in the blockade of Cadiz. It was during this period that perhaps my personal courage was more conspicuous than at any other period of my life. In an attack of the Spanish gunboats, I was boarded in my barge with its common crew of ten men, coxswain, Captain Fremantle, and myself, by the commander of the gunboats. The Spanish barge rowed twenty-six oars, besides officers, thirty in the whole; this was a service hand to hand with swords, in which my coxswain, John Sykes ... saved twice my life. Eighteen of the Spaniards being killed and several wounded, we succeeded in taking their commander.

St Vincent approved the attack, partly to place his fleet on the offensive. Reverberations from the Spithead and Nore mutinies had reached the fleet off Cadiz, and the admiral was fiercely determined to combat insurrection. Ireland had recently been subject to an abortive French invasion, and England was next expected to receive a landing. Apart from the Channel, all that stood between French and Spanish forces was the British fleet.

At the first signs of mutiny in the *St George* off Cadiz, St Vincent had the leaders court-martialled and executed. Because the trial did not end before sunset on Saturday 8 July, and he wanted immediate retribution, St Vincent had the executions carried out the following day, a Sunday, normally preserved from such abominations. Another vice-admiral opposed the action, but Nelson approved, congratulating St Vincent on finishing the business 'as it ought … even although it is a Sunday'. And he went further: 'Had it been Christmas Day instead of Sunday, I would have executed them.'

Another operation proposed by Nelson and sanctioned by St Vincent was an attack on the Spanish island of Tenerife, the landfall and watering-place for Spanish ships on the last stretch of their voyage home from the Caribbean with silver from the mines of Spanish America. The idea of seizing a Spanish treasure

BELOW: *Santa Cruz, Tenerife. In a letter outlining his plan of attack on the port, Nelson wrote that soldiers 'have not the same boldness in undertaking a practical measure that we have; we look to the benefit of our country, and wish our own fame every day to serve her: a soldier obeys his orders, and no more.'*

galleon had excited the British imagination for over 200 years. A galleon was expected at Tenerife.

Nelson proposed an attack on Santa Cruz, the port of the island. This St Vincent authorized in mid-July. With command over three ships of the line and four frigates, Nelson arranged a sudden landing of 1,000 men to the east of the town. However, the precipitate assault came to nothing. On Friday 21 July dawn revealed the boats of the squadron being swept along on a current in front of the town with a strong off-shore wind against them. Some landings were made but the shore was fortified and defended, and the British force was taken off the following night.

Surprise had been lost but, refusing to give up the attempt, Nelson planned a second assault for 24 July, himself taking personal command. Only the desire for honour, suitably cloaked in humility, justified both his own role and the suicidal nature of the plan. 'This night I, humble as I am, command the whole, destined to land under the batteries of the town,' he advised St Vincent, 'and tomorrow my head will probably be crowned with either laurel or cypress.'

This time the boats aimed straight for the harbour mole. Four or five did make their objective, 'but such a heavy fire of musketry and grape-shot was kept up ... that we could not advance, and we were nearly all killed or wounded'.

As Nelson himself attempted to land on the mole, he was hit by a musket ball in the right elbow. His stepson, Josiah Nisbet, was with him and promptly gathered him back into the boat, applied a tourniquet and ordered the boat back to the ships. Nelson recovered sufficiently to command the boat to pick up some men from a sinking cutter, then to steer for the *Theseus*. There Nelson's right arm was briskly amputated above the shattered elbow.

Meanwhile, the landing parties, amounting to no more than 700 men, were facing difficulties; for the garrison in Santa Cruz had been

ABOVE AND BELOW RIGHT: Memorandum written by Nelson from Tenerife, dated 20 July 1797, and a letter, dated 16 August 1797, written with his left hand after losing his right arm in the attack on Santa Cruz. In the letter he expressed the fear to St Vincent that 'a left-handed admiral will never again be considered as useful'.

RIGHT: Nelson wounded at Tenerife on 24 July 1797; the scene as portrayed by Richard Westall using written descriptions. Collapsing back into the boat as he tried to land, Nelson dropped his sword, which he then picked up in his left hand. His stepson Josiah Nisbet, standing behind, moved to support him.

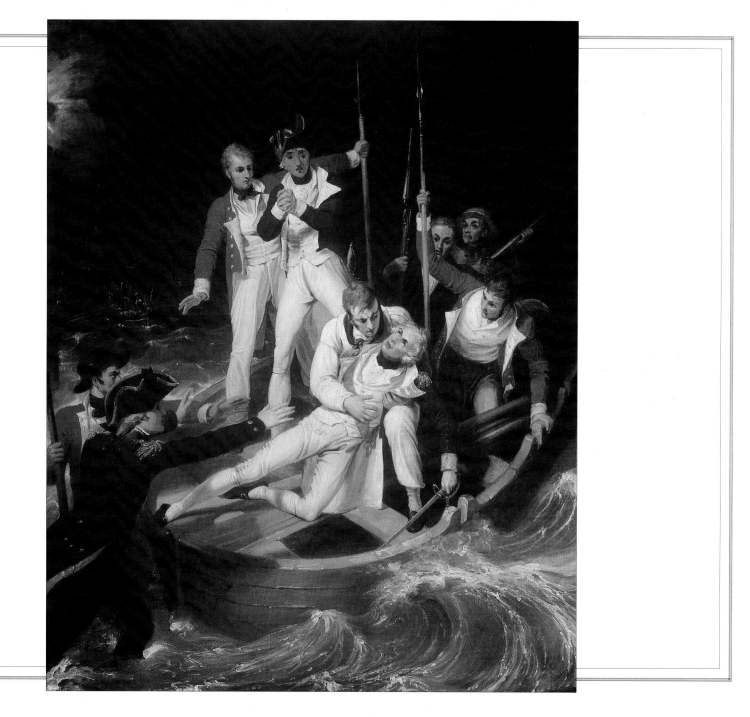

enlarged to 8,000. Eventually, after another night on shore and attempts to bluff the Spanish into surrender, the British force itself accepted terms by which it could return to the ships. One hundred and fifty-three men had been killed or lost; more would die of their wounds later.

After the attack Nelson despaired at the loss of his right arm. He wrote to St Vincent on 27 July:

> I am become a burthen to my friends and useless to my country ... When I leave your command, I become dead to the world; I go hence, and am no more seen ... I hope you will be able to give me a frigate to convey the remains of my carcase to England. You will excuse my scrawl, considering it is my first attempt.

On 5 August, as the *Theseus* made its way back to Cadiz, he wrote to his wife:

> My dearest Fanny, I am so confident of your affection that I feel the pleasure you will receive will be equal whether my letter is wrote by my right hand or left. It was the chance of war and I have great reason to be thankful, and I know it will add much to your pleasure in finding that Josiah under God's providence was principally instrumental in saving my life. As to my health, it never was better and now I hope soon to return to you, and my country I trust will not allow me any longer to linger in want of that pecuniary assistance which I have been fighting the whole war to preserve to her. But I shall not be surprised to be neglected and forgot as probably I shall no longer be considered as useful. However I shall feel rich if I continue to enjoy your affection. The cottage is now more necessary than ever ...

He went on:

> I beg neither you or my father will think much of this mishap. My mind has long been made up to such an event. God bless you and believe me your most affectionate husband ...

St Vincent received him well:

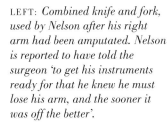

LEFT: *Combined knife and fork, used by Nelson after his right arm had been amputated. Nelson is reported to have told the surgeon 'to get his instruments ready for that he knew he must lose his arm, and the sooner it was off the better'.*

RIGHT: *Mezzotint engraved after the painting of Nelson by Lemuel Abbott and published in 1798. The portrait, one of 40 similar ones by Abbott, was painted from sketches done at Greenwich, where Nelson was recuperating. Fanny wrote of the picture, 'It is my companion, my sincere friend in your absence.'*

Mortals cannot command success; you and your companions have certainly deserved it, by the greatest degree of heroism and perseverence that ever was exhibited. I grieve for the loss of your arm, and ... will bow to your stump tomorrow morning, if you will give me leave.

From Cadiz Nelson sailed on for England, there to put the best gloss possible on his recent failure: 'success covers a multitude of blunders, and the want of it hides the greatest gallantry and good conduct.'

At last he was reunited with Fanny. He had been away for over four and a half years. Now she was able to nurse him; for, first in Bath, then in London, Nelson found his wound was not healing. Silk ligatures on the arteries had not come away and the wound was infected, swollen and painful.

Although suffering great misery from the wound, Nelson found his 'domestic happiness perfect'. Moreover, he was received well by 'John Bull' – the London crowd – and by the King, who invested him with the Order of the Bath at a levee towards the end of September 1797. He was painted by Lemuel Abbott, and a change in his appearance was apparent. His dry, frizzy hair was now almost white; missing teeth meant that his cheeks were sunken, and that he kept his lips together when he smiled to conceal their absence; his right eye was fixed, dim and milky blue in colour; and the sleeve of his missing right arm was pinned across his chest.

When Lady Spencer, the wife of the First Lord of the Admiralty, met him, she thought him a 'most uncouth creature'. 'He looked so sickly it was painful to see him.' None the less, she was impressed by the way he spoke and invited him and Fanny to dinner. In his reply to the invitation, he praised Fanny's 'angelic tenderness' and attention to his physical

needs. Indeed, when they attended the dinner, Nelson appeared devoted to her: 'he handed her to dinner and sat by her ... saying that he was so little with her that he would not voluntarily lose an instant of her society'. Together, they bought at last their 'cottage' – a house called Roundwood, near Ipswich – which Fanny would furnish when Nelson returned to sea.

For by December Nelson had recovered. In London he attended St George's church, Hanover Square, and recorded his 'Thanks to Almighty God for his perfect recovery from a severe wound'. Soon afterwards he was again appointed to St Vincent's fleet, to go out in the 74-gun *Vanguard*. As his health returned, his irritation with Fanny's inefficiencies in packing and sending his possessions resumed.

In May 1798 he was 'exhilarated beyond description' on being sent back into the Mediterranean with a squadron of ships to investigate the destination of an expeditionary force equipping at Toulon under General Bonaparte, with 15 ships of the line under the French admiral Brueys.

Off Toulon, a heavy storm on 19 to 20 May wreaked havoc in the British squadron, which found on regaining its station that the French had already sailed. Early June brought news that Nelson's squadron would be reinforced, bringing it up to 13 ships of the line; also that the French fleet had been sighted sailing south-east, possibly for Naples, or Malta, or even for Egypt, the stepping-stone for an assault on India.

Nelson followed, his reinforcements joining the squadron as he wrote ahead for information and assistance to Sir William Hamilton in Naples. Writing also to Lady Hamilton, whom he had not seen for five years, he received a strangely intimate response:

> God bless you and send you victorious and that I may see you bring back
> Bonaparte with you ... I shall be a fever of anxiety ... I will not say how glad
> I shall be to see you. Indeed I cannot describe to you my feelings of your
> being so near us.

ABOVE: *Cartoon by James Gillray entitled 'Fighting for the Dunghill: or Jack Tar settling Buonaparte', representing the struggle to overcome Napoleon's attempts to dominate Europe.*

RIGHT: *Imaginary view of the taking of Malta by the French fleet. Nelson received news of it as he sailed through the Straits of Messina. He told Sir William Hamilton that it was essential to 'have a free use of Sicily, to enable us to starve the French in Malta ... The King of Naples may now have a part in the glory in destroying these pests of the human race.'*

Although he exchanged letters at Naples, Nelson did not go on shore but sailed
on through the Straits of Messina. There, a Genoese brig gave him news that
the French had taken Malta from the Knights of the Order of St John of
Jerusalem and had then continued eastward. From all the information he could
gather, the French fleet's most probable destination was Egypt. Nelson thus
pressed on for Alexandria.

At the end of June, having scoured the Egyptian coastline, he could find no
trace of the enemy fleet. Cruising north, then west, he searched the eastern
Mediterranean and retraced his course to Syracuse in Sicily, but still there was

no sign of it. Casting around, he again heard, from the Greek town of Koroni in the Gulf of Messenia, that the French had been seen heading for Egypt. This time, off Alexandria, Nelson found the fleet of French transports, and further along the coast, moored in line ahead across the shallows of Aboukir Bay, the French fleet.

In the British fleet the excitement was intense. Nelson recounted how, when he saw the French, he could not help popping his head every now and then out of the window – even though he had a toothache.

There were 16 French warships at anchor. Although the sun was setting, Nelson made the signal to prepare for battle and that it was his intention to attack the enemy's van and centre as they lay there, according to plans previously discussed with his captains. Each British ship took soundings as she followed the *Goliath* and *Zealous* into the bay. Even so, the *Culloden*, commanded by Thomas Troubridge, grounded on shoals and lay stranded, prey to French guns on an island off Aboukir Point. The others steered in, realizing that as the French were moored only by the bow, there must be sufficient depth of water all round for them to swing at their anchors. If this was the case there was room for the British to outflank them, 'double' their line and attack from the landward as well as seaward side.

On the landward side the French were unprepared for fighting. With some British ships going behind the French and some remaining to seaward, the Battle of the Nile developed as night fell. Throughout the night, concentrating their force on key French vessels, then moving on to others further up the line, the twelve British ships of the line systematically battered ten French battleships into submission.

At 10 p.m. *L'Orient*, Admiral Brueys's flagship, blew up after fire reached her magazine. 'A most grand and awful spectacle', the detonation and shock reduced the guns of friend and

BELOW: *The French* Tonnant *and the English* Majestic *exchanging fire during the Battle of the Nile. In the* Tonnant *the French captain, who lost both legs and an arm, is being put into a tub of bran, from which he continued to direct action until he died.*

enemy alike to stunned silence for several minutes. Only two French ships of the line escaped, by cutting their cables and getting out to sea.

Nelson himself was again wounded. A fragment of metal slashed open his forehead, the deluge of blood at first making him think he was killed. But in the surgeon's cockpit on the orlop deck he was able to recover sufficiently to begin his report, and later to return on deck when *L'Orient* caught fire. About midnight the battle petered out, the British crews falling asleep where they had fought. Next morning 'the whole bay was covered with dead bodies, mangled, wounded and scorched, not a bit of clothes on them but their trousers'.

Over 3,000 Frenchmen were killed and wounded, with 3,000 seamen taken prisoner; the casualties were six times heavier than those of the British. It was a spectacular victory. Not only had the French army ashore been marooned in Egypt but their Mediterranean fleet had been destroyed, and the British had regained command of the Mediterranean. At a stroke the course of the Revolutionary war was altered.

Leaving some British vessels off Egypt, Nelson in the *Vanguard* made for Naples. The ship was desperately in need of dockyard attention, while he himself was suffering the after-effects of his new wound: splitting headaches and nausea, with some malarial bouts of fever.

As news of the battle and its effects spread across Europe, the response came back to Nelson in a growing flood of ecstatic congratulation. From Naples, to which two officers had been sent ahead, Emma Hamilton could hardly contain her delight:

> I am delirious with joy and assure you I have a fever
> caused by agitation and pleasure. Good God what a victory!
> Never, never has there been anything half so glorious, half
> so complete ... I fainted when I heard the joyful news
> and fell on my side and am hurt, but what of that ...

BELOW: *Nelson giving command of the* Vanguard *to Captain Berry after receiving a head wound. He reported to St Vincent, 'The support and assistance I have received from Captain Berry cannot be sufficiently expressed.'*

EMMA

EMILY LYON, as Emma was originally called, was born in 1765, the daughter of a blacksmith from the Wirral, in Cheshire. She was put to work as a nursery-maid, and first found employment in London in the household of Thomas Linley, a composer. By the age of 14 she was employed in a house in Arlington Street by Mrs Kelly, the 'madam' of a brothel. Rumour had it that she was soon the mistress of a naval officer, Captain John Willet Payne – a friend of the Prince of Wales – and an attendant in a Temple of Health and Hymen, where infertile couples could use a 'Grand celestial Bed' and conceive children 'as even the barren must do when so powerfully agitated in the delights of love'.

By the time she was 16, she had been moved to a cottage near Uppark, in Sussex, as mistress to Sir Harry Featherstonhaugh. There Emma gave birth to a child and met Charles Greville. When Featherstonhaugh tired of her, Greville installed her in London as 'the fair tea-maker of Edgeware Row', and she changed her name to Emma Hart.

All went well until Greville found an heiress who he thought would make him a suitable wife. Somehow he had to dispose of Emma. His mind turned to his uncle, Sir William Hamilton, whose first wife had died in 1782: 'by placing her within your reach, I render a necessity –

ABOVE: *Emma was a known beauty, much sought after as a model by fashionable artists. This picture of Emma was painted by George Romney while she was living under the protection of Charles Greville.*

which would otherwise be heartbreaking – tolerable and even comforting'.

'There is a great difference between her being with you or with me', Sir William replied from Naples, 'for she really loves you when she could only esteem and suffer me ... I do assure you when I was in England, tho' her exquisite beauty had frequently its effects on me, it would never have come into my head to have proposed a freedom beyond an innocent kiss.'

Greville persisted. He had never known anyone so 'completely led by good nature'; a 'cleanlier, sweeter bedfellow did not exist'. Eventually Sir William agreed to a temporary arrangement, and Emma, accompanied by her mother, arrived in Naples early in 1786. When Greville did not join them, Emma was desperately unhappy but soon resigned herself to the pleasure of Sir William's attentions. She was painted, had singing lessons, went to the opera, acted as hostess at formal dinners and began performing her 'Attitudes', or poses, before invited audiences.

After a time she moved into the rooms where Sir William lived and became his lover. 'As to Sir W.,' she wrote to Greville, 'I confess to you I doat on him, nor I never can love any other person but him. This confession will please you I know.'

I should feel it a glory to die in such a cause. No, I would not like to die until I see and embrace the *Victor of the Nile* ... Sir William is ten years younger since the happy news ... My dress from head to foot is *alla Nelson*. Even my shawl is in blue with gold anchors all over. My earrings are Nelson's anchors; in short, we are all be-Nelsoned ... I wish you could have seen our house, the three nights of illuminations. 'Tis, 'twas covered with your glorious name. There were three thousand lamps and there should have been three million.

Sir William Hamilton was welcoming, writing that 'a pleasant apartment is ready for you in my house and Emma is looking out for the softest pillows to repose the few wearied limbs you have left.'

Later, from London, came reports of similar delight and celebration. Lady Spencer was as ecstatic as Emma:

Joy, joy, joy to you, brave, gallant, immortalised Nelson! May the great God, whose cause you so valiantly support, protect and bless you to the end of your brilliant career! ... My heart is absolutely bursting ... This moment, the guns are firing, illuminations are preparing, your gallant name is echoed from street to street.

Only Fanny at Roundwood remained anxious and restrained:

The newspapers have tormented and almost killed me in regard to the desperate action you have fought with the French fleet. How human faculties

ABOVE: *Enamel patch box with a scene of the Battle of the Nile and the date 1 August 1798.*

BELOW: *Ribbons celebrating Nelson's victory were among the commemorative wares manufactured by the haberdashery trade.*

ABOVE: *Derby porcelain mug decorated with a copy of the gold medal struck by Nelson's prize-agent, Alexander Davison, to commemorate the Battle of the Nile.*

can be brought to make others intentionally miserable I cannot conceive. In my opinion a news paper writer, or a fabricator for them, is a despicable creature bearing a human shape. I trust in God for a continuance of his protection over you and to grant my dear husband a happy return to me and our good father, who has exerted his spirits pretty well.

Even after receiving news of the victory and Nelson's safety, she did not give way to joy, nor did she grasp the significance of the battle for Europe. She remained immersed in domestic matters, preoccupied with the duties the new house had brought her.

By the time Nelson received Fanny's response, he was experiencing pleasures of which he had previously had but a brief taste. The festivities in Naples would have turned the head of any successful officer far less susceptible to honours and flattery than Nelson. He had been wounded and was still feeling tired and ill. He had been deprived of the pleasures of female company for months and had probably never known such a person as Emma who, though in early middle age and growing fat, possessed beauty, sensuality and a taste for the theatrical that she used to please her male admirers. He was soon entranced.

Nelson wrote to Fanny describing his reception in Naples:

September 25th: The poor *Vanguard* arrived here on the 22nd. I must endeavour to convey to you something of what passed, but, if it was so affecting to those only who are united in bonds of friendship, what must it be to my dearest wife. My friends say everything which is most dear to me in the world. Sir William and Lady Hamilton came out to sea attended by numerous boats with emblems etc. My most respectable friends had really been laid up and seriously ill, first from anxiety and then from joy. It was imprudently told Lady Hamilton in a moment. The effect was a shot. She fell apparently dead and is not perfectly recovered from severe bruises. Alongside my honoured friends came, the scene in the boat appeared terribly affecting. Up

LEFT: *An Italian who watched Emma performing her 'Attitudes' remarked, 'she single-handedly created a living gallery of statues and paintings. I have never seen anything more fluid and graceful, more sublime and heroic.' An etching by Tommaso Piroli after one of Friedrich Rehberg's drawings.*

RIGHT: *Fanciful print of Nelson at the Neapolitan court crowned with a wreath of laurels. Emma wrote, 'The King and Queen adore him, and if he had been their brother, they could not have shown him more respect and attention.'*

flew her ladyship and exclaiming: '*Oh God is it possible*' fell into my arms more dead than alive. Tears however soon set matters to rights, when alongside came the King [Ferdinand]. The scene was in its way affecting. He took me by the hand, calling me his deliverer and preserver, with every other expression of kindness. In short all Naples calls me '*Nostra Liberatore*'.

He went on to reveal something of his feelings for Lady Hamilton:

I hope one day to have the pleasure of introducing you to Lady Hamilton. She is one of the very best women in this world. How few could have made the turn she has. She is an honour to her sex and a proof that even reputation may be regained, but I own it requires a great soul. Her kindness, with Sir William, to me is more than I can express. I am in their house, and I may now tell you it required all the kindness of my friends to set me up. Her ladyship, if Josiah was to stay, would make something of him, and with all his bluntness I am sure he likes Lady Hamilton more than any female. She would fashion him in 6 months in spite of himself. I believe Lady Hamilton intends writing you.

Three days later he wrote of the festivities that were being planned:

> The preparations of Lady Hamilton for celebrating my birthday tomorrow are enough to fill me with vanity. Every ribbon every button has 'Nelson' etc., the whole service are 'H. N. Glorious 1st August'. Songs, sonnets are numerous beyond what I ever could deserve. I send the additional verse to 'God save the King' as I know you will sing it with pleasure. I cannot move on foot or in a carriage for the kindness of the populace, but good Lady Hamilton preserves all the papers as the highest treat for you. The Queen yesterday being still ill sent her favourite son to visit and bring me a letter from her of gratitude and thanks.

A week later Nelson described the birthday celebrations to her:

> Could I, my dear Fanny, tell you half the honours which are done me here not a ream of paper would hold the heads. On my birthday night 80 people dined at Sir William's, 1,740 came to a ball, 800 supped, conducted in such a style of elegance as I never saw or shall again probably. A rostral column is erected under a magnificent canopy, never Lady Hamilton says to come down while they remain in Naples. My father will tell you all about it. In the front, Nelson. On the pedestal 'veni vidi vici', anchors, inscriptions ...

Among the gifts he received was a jewelled plume of triumph, or *chelengk*, to be worn on a turban: this came with other jewelled items from the Sultan of

ABOVE: *Miniature of Emma after a painting by Madame Vigée-Lebrun. It originally belonged to Sir William and was bequeathed by him to Nelson, who kept it always with him.*

RIGHT: *View of Posilippo by John Thomas Serres, possibly with Nelson and Lady Hamilton. Vesuvius is in the background, with a two-decker British man-of-war and a Neapolitan galley in the bay.*

Ottoman Turkey. In England he was created a baron, a disappointment as he had been hoping for a viscountcy. Emma wrote with indignation:

> If I was King of England I would make you the most noble, puissant Duke Nelson, Marquis Nile, Earl Alexandria, Viscount Pyramid, Baron Crocodile, and Prince Victory that posterity might have you in all forms.

Under the romantic influence cast by Emma, Nelson wrote to St Vincent:

> I am writing opposite Lady Hamilton, therefore you will not be surprised at the glorious jumble of this letter. Were your lordship in my place, I much doubt if you could write so well: our hearts and hands must be all in a flutter: Naples is a dangerous place and we must keep clear of it.

He was indeed quickly frustrated with political life in Naples, observing to St Vincent as he planned a cruise to Malta:

> I trust, my Lord, in a week we shall be at sea. I am very unwell and the miserable conduct of this Court is not likely to cool my irritable temper. It is a country of fiddlers and poets, whores and scoundrels.

Yet, with only a few absences at sea, Nelson was to remain in Naples, with or close to the Hamiltons, for over a year and a half.

His attachment to Emma grew, and it was all too obvious to others. While reviewing the Neapolitan army with the Queen and Emma, he was reported to have sat beside the latter in a horse-drawn chariot 'fascinated and submissive to her charms'. The adulation must also have been conveyed to Fanny, to whom he praised Emma as a 'wonderful' influence on Josiah. It was a relationship that was to worry not only Fanny but those who relied on Nelson's judgement as a naval officer.

LEFT: *Engraving after a large-scale drawing presented to Nelson on his arrival at Naples on 22 September 1798. The various devices are emblematic of victory at the Battle of the Nile and of the bravery of the officers and men who took part in it.*

CHAPTER SIX

HONOUR AND DISREPUTE

ABOVE: *Queen Maria Carolina.
'She is quick, clever, insinuating
when she pleases, loves and hates
violently,' was the opinion of Sir
William's first wife. 'Her strongest
and most durable passions are
ambition and vanity.'*

AFTER THE BATTLE OF THE NILE Nelson was given responsibility for all naval operations east of Corsica and Sardinia, including the blockade of the French in Malta and Egypt. For these two purposes he despatched small squadrons under Captain Hood and Captain Ball, while he managed his command from Naples.

There, the government was in a critical state of indecision. Early in 1798 the French had seized Rome, deposed the Pope, and established their own republic. King Ferdinand was exposed to invasion and had an army prepared to advance on Rome. But to do this he and Queen Maria Carolina had to abandon their neutrality and, as Sir William Hamilton urged, ally themselves with Britain, Austria and Russia.

Nelson's presence thus became invaluable to the Neapolitan and the allied cause. His military opinion was deeply respected, while his ships could provide practical assistance to the Neapolitan army. Early in October he wrote to Emma:

> My dear Madam, I cannot be an indifferent spectator to what has and is passing in the Two Sicilies, nor to the misery which (without being a politician) I cannot but see plainly is ready to fall on these kingdoms, now so loyal, by the worst of all policy – that of procrastination ... Has not the uniform conduct of the French been to lull governments into a false security, and to destroy them? ... Is it not known to every person that Naples is the next marked object for plunder? With this knowledge, and that his Sicilian Majesty has an army ready (I am told) to march into a country anxious to receive them, with the advantage of carrying the war from, instead of waiting for it at home, I am all astonished that the army has not marched a month ago.

ABOVE: *Ferdinand IV, King of
Naples and Sicily. 'The chase in
winter and parties of sailing or
fishing in summer call out His
Majesty every day at sun rising
and keep him out till it sets', Sir
William wrote.*

RIGHT: *Arrival of the French
army in Naples, 21 January 1799.*

BELOW: *Mourning locket containing a lock of Prince Alberto's hair. The six-year-old son of the King and Queen died in Emma's arms on the voyage from Naples to Palermo.*

With the arrival of an Austrian general to lead the army, Nelson arranged to land troops at Leghorn to the north of Rome, to cut the French lines of communication and retreat. At first all went well. Nelson carried out his part in the operation late in November 1798; the French withdrew, Rome was occupied by Neapolitan troops and King Ferdinand invited the Pope to return. But in mid-December the reinforced French army invaded Neapolitan territory and Nelson had to evacuate the royal family with the Hamiltons to Palermo, in Sicily.

After a stormy voyage, during which a six-year-old royal prince died in Emma's arms, the party disembarked the day after Christmas. Nelson took up residence in the *palazzo* occupied by the Hamiltons. There, in the early months of 1799, after Emma had performed her poses – or 'Attitudes' as she described them – for guests, or enjoyed gambling with Nelson weary at her elbow, they became sexually involved. Nelson was still ill with headaches, nausea, digestive trouble and spasms of pain in his chest. All were partly induced by worry,

ABOVE: *Lady Hamilton performing her 'Attitudes' by P. A. Novelli. She could change from a romantic figure to one of saintly devotion by the simple act of rearranging her long shawl. 'Sir William is never so happy as when he is pointing out my beauties to his friends', she wrote.*

and his relationship with Emma probably added to the problem. That he was troubled by the development was reflected in his communications with Fanny. He felt both unable to write much to her or to receive her, should she follow advice to try to visit him:

> You must not think it possible for me to write even to you as much I used to do. In truth, I have such quantities of writing public letters that my private correspondence has been, and must continue to be, greatly neglected. You would by February have seen how unpleasant it would have been had you followed *any* advice, which carried you from England to a wandering sailor. I could, if you had come, *only* have struck my flag, and carried you back again, for it would have been impossible to have set up an establishment at either Naples or Palermo. Nothing but the situation of the country has kept me from England; and if I have the happiness of seeing their Sicilian Majesties safe on their throne again, it is probable I shall yet be home in the summer. Good Sir William, Lady Hamilton, and myself, are the mainsprings of the machine which manage what is going on in this country. We are all bound to England when we can quit our posts with propriety.

In April 1799 a French fleet of 25 ships of the line escaped from Brest and entered the Mediterranean, followed by 17 Spanish ships from Cadiz. Lord St Vincent was sick ashore at Gibraltar. Lord Keith, who had been blockading Cadiz, pursued the French and demanded immediate reinforcement. Nelson despatched ten ships of the line to Keith at Minorca but declined to leave Palermo himself. He informed St Vincent on 12 May:

> You may depend on my exertion and I am only sorry that I cannot move to your help: but this island appears to hang on my stay. Nothing could console the Queen this night but my promise not to leave them unless the battle was to be fought off Sardinia.

ABOVE: *Sonnet in Italian transcribed for Nelson and addressed to Lady Hamilton, expressing his sincere admiration.*

RIGHT: *Border from a dress worn by Lady Hamilton in 1799 at a fête in Palermo. The title of Duke of Brontë, together with a 30,000-acre estate in Sicily, was conferred on Nelson by King Ferdinand in August 1799.*

The following day Nelson expressed his dilemma at having to choose between going himself to assist Keith and remaining to influence the situation in Italy and the alliance against France. He again wrote to St Vincent:

> Should you come upwards without a battle, I hope in that case you will afford me an opportunity of joining you; for my heart would break to be near my Commander-in-Chief and not assisting him in such a time. What a state I am in! If I go, I risk, and more than risk, Sicily, and what is now safe on the Continent; for we know from experience that more depends on *opinion* than on acts themselves. As I stay, my heart is breaking; and to mend the matter, I am seriously unwell.

St Vincent appreciated the difficulty, for situated off southern Italy Nelson could cover the approaches to Malta and Egypt as well as to Sicily. Even while they exchanged letters, however, Nelson's military choices were suddenly extended as civil war erupted in Naples. A senior priest, Cardinal Ruffo, had been selected by the King to raise resistance to the French occupation and the new 'Parthenopean Republic' they had founded. Ruffo needed reinforcements to succeed.

Nelson sent four ships and was begged by the Queen and Lady Hamilton to go himself. He could not resist the request and, taking Sir William and Lady Hamilton on board with him, returned to Naples. There, Ruffo's 'troops' were pillaging the houses of intellectuals and gentlemen as punishment for their alleged sympathies with the French and local Jacobins, leaving their dead bodies stripped naked in the streets. To gain a measure of control, Ruffo had agreed an

RIGHT: *One of several versions of Leonardo Guzzardi's portrait of Nelson, painted in Naples in 1798-9. He wears the gold Nile medal and in his hat the* chelengk, *or plume, with 13 strands of diamonds and in the middle 'a radiant star ... turning on its centre by means of watch-work, which winds up behind'. It was presented to him by the Sultan after his victory at the Battle of the Nile.*

LEFT: *Insignia of the Neapolitan Order of St Ferdinand. The order was devised by King Ferdinand IV for Nelson, and otherwise restricted to members of the royal family. Bearers were entitled to wear their hats in the presence of the king.*

armistice and accepted the surrender of the French troops on humane terms.

Nelson refuted the terms, as not having been agreed by the King, and precipitated another outbreak of indiscriminate violence. He supplied muskets to those who claimed to support Ruffo and sent marines on shore with royal troops. The French garrison was finally overcome, and a prolonged period of trials and executions of Neapolitan 'traitors' started. Nelson himself had the head of the Neapolitan navy, Francesco Caracciolo, Duke of Brienza, tried by court-martial and hanged.

As the orgy of revenge subsided into systematic repression, Nelson was called away by Lord Keith, now commander-in-chief in the Mediterranean. Minorca was still under threat from the French and Keith requested him to take command of the defence of the island, a key British base for the blockade of Toulon. Although, at the third strongly worded request, he sent ships, Nelson himself refused to go. He still maintained that it was better to risk Minorca than to leave the Two Sicilies. But his service to the Neapolitan royal family had become personal: at the King's request, he immediately carried him back to Palermo.

For his support, Nelson was given the given the dukedom of Brontë in Sicily and began to sign himself 'Nelson & Brontë'. Lord Elgin, passing through Palermo on his way to Constantinople, remarked that Nelson now 'looks very old, has lost his upper teeth, sees ill of one eye and has a film coming over both of them'. His responsibilities increased in August 1799 when Lord Keith pursued the French and Spanish fleets back through the Straits of Gibraltar and left Nelson in command of the whole of the British Mediterranean fleet.

Life with the Hamiltons was becoming strained. Sir William complained that he bore the expense of entertaining

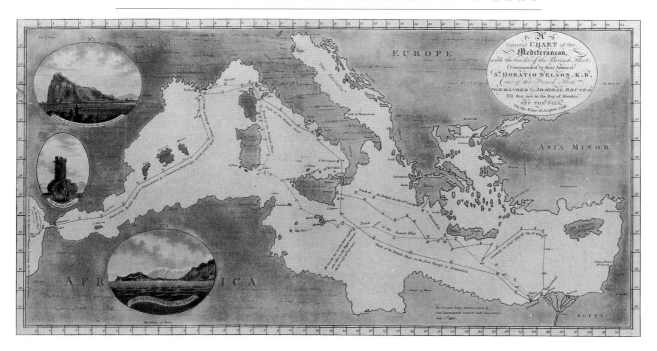

many naval visitors and was becoming conscious of the deepening relationship
of Nelson and Emma. For some time they had been lovers, but now Nelson
could hardly bear to be apart from her. This was evident in January, when Lord
Keith demanded Nelson met him at Leghorn and accompanied him back to
Palermo. There Keith described 'a scene of fulsome vanity and absurdity'.

Returning from Leghorn at the end of January 1800 Nelson wrote Emma a
long love letter (reproduced here in part, in its original form):

> Wednesday 29th Janry: Separated from all I hold dear in this world what is
> the use of living if indeed such an existence can be called so, nothing could
> alleviate such a separation but the call of our Country but loitering time away
> with nonsense is too much, no Separation no time my only beloved Emma can
> alter my love and affection for You ... Continue only to love Your faithful

LEFT: *'General Chart of the Mediterranean, with the tracks of the British fleet ... and of the French fleet ... Till they met in the Bay of Aboukir, off the Nile.'* In February 1800 Nelson, in the Foudroyant, *captured* Le Généreux, *one of the two French ships surviving from the Battle of the Nile; the other one was taken a month later.*

Nelson as he loves his Emma. You are my guide I submit to You, let me find all My fond heart hopes and wishes with the risk of my life i have been faithful to my word never to partake of any amusement or sleep on Shore.

On Thursday the letter continued:

We have been Six days from Leghorn and no prospect of our making a passage to Palermo, to me it is worse than death. I can neither Eat or Sleep for thinking of You my dearest love, I never touch even pudding You know the reason. No I would Starve sooner ...

And the following day:

I shall run mad we have had a gale of Wind that is nothing but I am 20 Leagues farther from You than Yesterday noon. Was I master notwithstanding the weather I would have been 20 Leagues nearer but my Commander In Chief knows not what I feel by absence, last Night I did nothing but dream of You altho' I woke 20 times in the Night. In one of my dreams I thought I was at a large Table You was not present, Sitting between a Princess who I detest and another. They both tried to Seduce Me and the first wanted to take those liberties with Me which no Woman in this World but Yourself ever did. The consequence was I knocked her down and in the moment of bustle you came in and taking Me in Your embrace wispered I love nothing but You My Nelson. I kissed You fervently And we enjoy'd the height of love. Ah Emma I pour out my Soul to you. If you love any thing but Me You love those who feel not like your N.

On Sunday it concluded:

Fair wind which makes me a little better in hopes of seeing You my love My Emma to morrow. Just 138 Miles distant, and I trust to find You like myself, for no love is like Mine towards You.

Nelson's resentment of his superior officer was apparent in the note he wrote to Emma immediately on reaching Palermo:

3 February 1800. My Dear Lady Hamilton, Having a Commander in Chief, I cannot come on shore till I have made *my manners* to him. Times are changed; but, if he does not come on shore directly, I will not wait.

From Palermo Lord Keith insisted that Nelson accompany him to Malta. On the way Nelson's ship took the French *Le Généreux*, which had escaped from Aboukir Bay in 1798. The action was specially satisfying in view of his subordinate relationship to Keith. Off Valetta, on 20 February, the mutual antipathy of the two officers was made clear in a letter to Emma:

> Had you seen the Peer receive me, I know not what you would have done; but I can guess. But never mind! I told him, that I had made a vow, if I took the *Généreux* by myself, it was my intention to strike my flag. To which he made no answer ... My head aches dreadfully, and I have none here to give me moment's comfort.

Keith wanted to leave Nelson in command off Malta, but Nelson claimed his state of health made it impossible to remain and insisted on returning to his 'friends in Palermo'. On hearing this, Lord Spencer, First Lord of the Admiralty, advised him to come home rather than remain inactive at a foreign court. As the Hamiltons were also returning to England, Nelson seized the opportunity of resigning his command.

The party began their journey back to England from Leghorn. Emma's mother, who had always been present in the background, came too, making them a group of four, apart from their servants. Emma was now pregnant by Nelson and suffering nausea, a problem Sir William, in true diplomatic fashion, appeared to ignore. Keith had refused to let Nelson take them all the way home in a warship; at Leghorn Emma decided she could not tolerate the discomfort of the sea voyage at all. To avoid the French, their journey overland took them through Florence, Trieste, Klagenfurt and Vienna to Prague, where they embarked on a barge for an 11-day passage down the Elbe

LEFT: *Pastel portrait of Nelson by Johann Heinrich Schmidt, Court Painter to the Elector of Saxony, done while he, the Hamiltons and Emma's mother were travelling back to England. In Dresden he appeared at court 'a perfect constellation of stars and orders'.*

RIGHT: *Schmidt's portrait of Lady Hamilton, done at the same time as the one of Nelson. In Dresden it was noted that 'in spite of the accuracy of her imitation of the finest ancient draperies, her usual dress is tasteless, vulgar, loaded and unbecoming'.*

river to Dresden and Hamburg. At Dresden both Emma and Nelson had their portraits painted by Johann Heinrich Schmidt, who produced perhaps the most intimate images of the two that were ever painted; that of Emma, Nelson thereafter always carried with him on board ship.

The journey through Europe was marked by local festivities celebrating Nelson and his victories wherever they went. Some who saw them remarked on the curiosity of Nelson's appearance, his vanity, and the gross size, coarse language and behaviour of Emma. Few failed to notice the closeness of the couple, to which Sir William was a gentle onlooker. At Vienna:

> Lady Hamilton never stopped talking, singing, laughing, gesticulating and mimicking while the favoured son of Neptune appeared to leave her no more than did her shadow, trying to meet with his own small eyes the great orbs of his beloved and, withal, as motionless and silent as a monument, embarrassed by his poor figure and by all the emblems, cords and crosses with which he was bedecked.

An observer at Prague remarked that he:

> was one of the most insignificant figures I ever saw in my life ... a more miserable collection of bones and wizened frame I have yet to come across ... Lady Hamilton behaved like a loving sister towards him; led him, often took hold of his hand, whispered something into his ear, and he twisted his mouth into the faintest resemblance of a smile ...

To another in Dresden Nelson seemed:

> a little man, without dignity ... Lady Hamilton takes possession of him, and he is a willing captive, the most submissive and devoted I have ever seen. Sir William is old, unfirm, all admiration of his wife [sic] and never spoke ... but to applaud her ...

From Hamburg they expected to receive passage from a Royal Navy frigate, but no naval vessel arrived and they took a packet boat for Great Yarmouth on the Norfolk coast. The party reached England on 6 November 1800, and three days later Nelson was finally reunited with Fanny in London at Nerot's Hotel in King Street, St James's. It was a strained meeting, with the Hamiltons in the background and Nelson's father there too. The press had already made much of Nelson's affair with Emma: Rowlandson, Gillray and the elder Cruikshank had all produced caricatures, and polite society was deciding how it would treat the adulterous admiral and his mistress. That same day Lord St Vincent, then commanding the Channel fleet, observed to Sir Evan Nepean, Secretary at the Admiralty:

> It is evident from Lord Nelson's letter to you on his landing that he is doubtful of the propriety of his conduct – I have no doubt he is pledged to getting Lady

BELOW: *The Norfolk port of Great Yarmouth, where the party arrived by mail packet on 6 November 1800. Nelson was greeted by a jubilant crowd and sworn in as a freeman of the borough. 'I am a Norfolk man,' he proclaimed, 'and glory in being so.'*

H received at St James's and every where, and that he will get into much brouillerie about it.

And indeed, at a royal levee the King virtually snubbed Nelson, the latter being tactless enough to attend wearing his Turkish and Neapolitan decorations as well as the Order of the Bath. Sir John Moore, the distinguished army officer (who was later to die a hero's death at Corunna), observed that Nelson appeared 'more like a Prince of the Opera than the Conqueror of the Nile. It is really melancholy to see a brave and good man, who has deserved well of his country, cutting so pitiful a figure.'

However, it was a figure the general public loved. Nelson continued to be fêted wherever he went. On the way to the Lord Mayor's Banquet his coach was dragged up Ludgate Hill by the crowd; he was cheered at the theatre and was dined by the East India Company and by Alexander Davison. The latter, whom he had first met at Quebec, and who acted as his prize-agent, introduced him to William Pitt, the Prime Minister.

Nelson attended some of the official banquets in his honour without Fanny. But at a more private occasion Lady Spencer noted that, though Fanny behaved in exemplary fashion, Nelson treated her 'with every mark of dislike, and even of contempt'. Once, the Nelsons entertained the Hamiltons to dinner. The party disintegrated when Nelson suggested that Fanny assist Emma, who was still suffering sickness from her pregnancy. It was possibly that night that Nelson wandered the streets until four in the morning, ending at the Hamiltons' address to ask to live with them. He did, however, afterwards return to his own house and to Fanny.

Nelson and the Hamiltons, but not Fanny, received an invitation to spend Christmas of 1800 with the rich and eccentric William Beckford, at Fonthill in Wiltshire. Nelson returned to Fanny after Christmas, but they both now knew that their marriage was no more than a façade. After a quarrel about Lady Hamilton they parted. Nelson travelled with his brother William to Plymouth to take command of the *San Josef*, his Spanish prize taken at Cape St Vincent. From Southampton on 13 January 1801 he sent Fanny a friendly note:

ABOVE: *Detail from James Gillray's cartoon 'John Bull taking a Luncheon; or British Cooks, cramming Old Grumble-Gizzard, with Bonne Chere'. John Bull consuming yet another 'frigasée' represents the insatiable appetite of the British for victory.*

ABOVE: *Detail of Nelson offering John Bull a 'frigasée à la Nelson' on a plate, from the same cartoon. From his pocket hangs a 'List of French ships taken, burnt and destroyed'; behind is the grim face of Admiral Lord Howe, amid a group of other naval heroes.*

ABOVE: *Enamel pendant with a sailor and the words 'Nelson for Ever', produced at the time of his first appearance in England following his victory at the Battle of the Nile.*

RIGHT: *'The Hero of the Nile', a print by James Gillray emphasizing Nelson's frail and battered appearance, and his ostentation in wearing the* chelengk *and scarlet cloak presented to him by the Sultan.*

ABOVE: *Pendant decorated with the figure of a naval marine or sea-soldier standing in front of the scene of battle in Aboukir Bay, with French ships in flames. Made in about 1800.*

My dear Fanny, We are arrived, and heartily tired; and with kindest regards
to my father, believe me, your affectionate Nelson.

Neither Fanny nor Nelson knew they were not to meet again. For Nelson, it
was a time of crisis, to which his life for the past 18 months had been leading.
Unlike his previous crises, which had been military and largely of his own calculation, this was to be protracted and emotional. Socially ostracized, criticized and separated from those whom he loved, he attempted to maintain appearances. But to those who knew him, his misery was apparent. St Vincent attributed it to a disagreement he and Nelson had had over prize-money, which would eventually be settled in court. 'Nelson was very low when he first came here the day before yesterday,' he reported to Nepean, from Tor Abbey in Devon, on 15 January; he:

> appeared and acted as if he had done me
> an injury and felt apprehension that I was
> acquainted with it; poor man! he is
> devoured with vanity, weakness and folly,
> was strung with ribbons, medals, &c, and
> yet pretended that he wished to avoid the
> honours and ceremonies he everywhere
> met with upon the road.

LEFT: *'Nelson's Reception at Fonthill', from the* Gentleman's Magazine. *'Lord Nelson was loudly huzzaed by the multitude as he entered the first coach. They all proceeded slowly and in order, as the dusk of the evening was growing into darkness … soon after having entered the great wall, which includes the abbey-woods, the procession passed a noble Gothic arch.'*

Nelson's emotional state naturally affected the view senior naval officers took of him as one of themselves. Like Lord Keith, St Vincent generally disapproved of Nelson's behaviour, and maintained that he was unfit to lead a fleet that had major strategic responsibilities. St Vincent commanded the Channel Fleet, and in November 1800 he had observed to Nepean:

Troubridge says Lord Spencer talks of putting him in a two deck ship; if he
does, he must give him a separate command, for he cannot bear confinement
to any object; he is a partizan, his ship always in the most dreadful disorder,
and [he] never can become an officer fit to be placed where I am.

He recognized that Nelson's temperament was one that precipitated devastating, semi-suicidal battles, intimidating and overwhelming to an enemy. He thus
approved Nelson's appointment as second-in-command of a fleet equipping for
the Baltic under Sir Hyde Parker. He would, in St Vincent's view, 'act the fighting part well'.

The perceptions of senior officers such as St Vincent and Keith would
henceforward carry more weight, for in February 1801 St Vincent became First
Lord of the Admiralty. From this time, Nelson would be placed and managed as
an instrument of state. While war lasted, he would be employed at sea – as a
deterrent to the enemy. At the same time his own
personal needs would be ignored, and
deliberately so while he maintained
his association with Emma Hamilton,
which was provoking scandal that
was embarrassing to a prurient
and severe ministry needing all the
credibility it could muster. It was a situation
to which Nelson's own ambitions and person-
ality had brought him but one no easier for
him to endure because of that.

LEFT: *The very public love affair
of Nelson and Lady Hamilton
caricatured by Isaac Cruikshank.
Detail from a scene at the
Mansion House entitled 'Smoking
Attitudes'. Emma is depicted in
one of her Attitudes and Nelson
smokes a pipe that bears a
resemblance to one of Sir
William's antique finds.*

CHAPTER SEVEN

DEFIANCE AND DOMESTICITY

NELSON WAS SEPARATED FROM Emma just as she was about to give birth to his child. Their immediate difficulty became one of communicating. The manner in which they overcame the problem gave rise to a remarkable series of letters.

To carry their letters between Nelson's ship and Emma's residence in London, they trusted only Sir William's confidential secretary, James Oliver; and to convey their most intimate thoughts they invented the device of speaking about a seaman on board Nelson's ship, whom they named Thomson, and his lover or wife (it varied), befriended by Emma. Between these two they pretended to transmit messages out of kindness: the fictional characters became their most intimate selves. The pretence was tried for the first time at the beginning of 1801, when Emma's pregnancy was reaching its full term. On 26 January Nelson wrote from the *San Josef*, shortly before the ship moved to Tor Bay:

> I delivered poor Mrs Thomson's note; her friend is truly thankful for her
> kindness and your goodness. Who does not admire your benevolent heart.
> Poor man! he is very anxious, and begs you will, if she is not able, write a line
> just to comfort him. He appears to me to feel very much her situation; he is so
> agitated, and will be so for 2 or 3 days, that he says he cannot write, and that I
> must send his kind love and affectionate regards.

The following day Nelson's spirits were very low:

> I know nothing of my destination more than I did when in London, but the
> papers and reports of my being put in a bad ship which, although I can hardly

RIGHT: *The Battle of Copenhagen, 2 April 1801, a painting by Nicholas Pocock. Nelson disobeyed Admiral Hyde Parker's signal of recall and the fighting continued. A ceasefire was agreed as a result of Nelson's communiqué, which he directed 'To the brothers of Englishmen, the Danes'.*

credit, fills me with sorrow, which, joined to my private feelings, makes me this day ready to burst every moment into tears ... Mrs Thomson's friend is this moment come into my room. He desires me to thank you for your goodness to his friend. He appears almost as miserable as myself. He says you have always been kind to his dear Mrs Thomson, and he hopes you will continue your goodness to her on this trying occasion.

On 28 January his misery took a physical form:

BELOW: *Envelope addressed to Lady Hamilton, to whom Nelson wrote sometimes as many as four letters a day. Shortly before the birth of their daughter, they started communicating about the child using the pretence of writing on behalf of a sailor called Thomson and his sweetheart.*

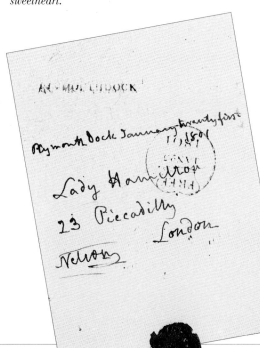

My eye is very bad. I have had the physician of the fleet to examine it. He has directed me not to write (and yet I am forced this day to write to Lord Spencer, St Vincent, Davison about my law-suit, Troubridge, Locker &c but you are the only female I write to); not to eat any thing but the most simple food; not to touch wine or porter; to sit in a dark room; to have green shades for my eyes – (will you, my dear friend, make me one or two? nobody else shall) – and to bathe them in cold water every hour. I fear it is the writing has brought on this complaint. My eye is like blood; and the film so extended, that I only see from the corner farthest from my eye. What a fuss about my complaints! But, being so far from my sincere friends, I have leisure to brood over them. I have this moment seen Mrs Thomson's friend. Poor fellow! he seems very uneasy and melancholy. He begs you to be kind to her; and I have assured him of your readiness to relieve the dear good woman ...

On 1 February, however, despondency turned to delight, for Emma had given birth to a daughter:

I believe poor dear Mrs Thomson's friend will go mad with joy. He cries, prays, and performs all tricks, yet dare not show all or any of his feelings, but he has only me to consult with. He swears he will drink your health this day in a bumper, and damn me if I don't join him in spite of all the doctors in Europe, for none regard you with truer affection than myself. You are a dear, good creature and your kindness and attentions to poor Mrs T stamps you higher than ever in my mind. I cannot write, I am so agitated by this young man at my elbow. I believe he is foolish; he does nothing but rave about you & her. I own I participate of his joy and cannot write anything.

Over the next few days Nelson became more practical, writing as though taking down a message from Thomson. On 3 February:

Your good and dear friend does not think it proper at present to write with his own hand but he hopes the time may not be far distant when he may be united for ever to the object of his wishes, his only, *only* love. He swears before heaven that he will marry you as soon as it is possible, which he fervently prays may be soon. He charges me to say how dear you are to him, and that you must, every opportunity, kiss and bless for him his dear little girl, which he wishes to be called Emma, out of gratitude to our dear, good Lady Hamilton; but in either, its from Lord N. he says, or Lady H., he leaves to your judgement and choice. I have given Lord N. a hundred pounds this morning, for which he will give Lady Hamilton an order on his agents; and I beg that you will distribute amongst those who have been useful to you on the late occasion; and your friend, my dear Mrs Thomson, may be sure of my care of him and his interest, which I consider as dearly as my own.

He then became concerned about the process of naming the child. Thus, on 5 February he wrote:

Your dear and excellent friend has desired me to say that it is not usual to christen children till they are a month or six weeks old; and as Lord Nelson will probably be in town, as well as myself, before we go to the Baltic, he proposes then, if you approve, to christen the child, and that myself and Lady Hamilton should be two of the sponsors. It can be christened at St George's, Hanover Square; and, I believe, the parents being at the time out of the

RIGHT: *Engraving of Nelson with a shade above his right eye. He lost the sight of this eye at the siege of Calvi in 1794, writing to Fanny, 'as to all the purpose of use, it is gone'. In January 1801, in a letter from the* San Josef, *he asked Emma to make him some green eyeshades to reduce glare.*

113

kingdom, if it is necessary, it can be stated born at Portsmouth or at sea. Its name will be Horatia, daughter of Johem and Moreta Etnorb. If you read the surname backwards, and take the letters of the other names, it will make, very extraordinary, the names of your real and affectionate friends, Lady Hamilton and myself; but, my dear friend, consult Lady Hamilton. Your friend consults me, and I would not lead him wrong for the world; he has not been very well: I believe he has fretted, but his spirit is too high to own it ... The child, if you like it, can be named by any clergyman without its going to church.

By degrees, through 'discussion' with Emma, he gave up the idea of immediately christening the child, now named Horatia, and concerned himself instead with financing the cost of a nurse for her, a Mrs Gibson in Little Titchfield Street. For neither Emma's lifestyle nor the position of Sir William Hamilton could brook the baby living under his roof.

Paradoxically, too, Nelson was obsessed by thoughts that the Prince of Wales might attempt to make Emma his mistress and was passionately jealous. Sir William felt some obligation to have the Prince to dinner, but Nelson protested to Emma:

> Sir William should say to the Prince that, situated as you are, it would be highly improper for you to admit H.R.H. That the Prince should wish it I am not surprized at, and that he will attempt every means to get into your house and into any place where you may dine. Sir Wm should speak out, and if the Prince is a man of honour he will quit the pursuit of you. I know his aim is to have you for a mistress. The thought so agitates me that I cannot write. I had wrote a few lines last night, but I am in tears, I cannot bear it.

Two weeks later, when the social engagement with the Prince was arranged, he was again distraught:

> I am so agitated that I can write nothing. I knew it would be so, and you can't help it. Why did you not tell Sir William? Your character will be gone. Do not

LEFT: *Nelson was distraught at the prospect of the Prince of Wales taking Emma as his mistress, were they to meet at Sir William's table. 'The thought so agitates me that I cannot write. I had wrote a few lines last night, but I am in tears, I cannot bear it.' In fact the meeting never did take place. This picture of the Prince is by Richard Cosway.*

Lady Nelson seated at a table with a bust of Nelson. 'Do, my Dear Husband, let us live together,' she wrote, 'I assure you again I have but one wish in the world, to please you.' Nelson never replied.

RIGHT: *Watercolour drawing of Nelson in 1802. He had once written to Fanny, 'my whole life shall ever be devoted to make you completely happy, whatever whims may sometimes take me.' This and the drawing of his wife are by Henry Edridge.*

have him *en famille*, the more the better. Do not sit long at table. Good God! he will be next you, and telling you soft things. If he does, tell it out at table, and turn him out of the house. Do not sit long. If you sing a song, I know you cannot help it, do not let him sit next you, but at dinner he will hob glasses with you ... I am gone almost mad, but you cannot help it. It will be in all the newspapers with hints.

Sir William wrote to Nelson to calm his fears and assure him that every precaution would be taken to keep the event quiet and avoid scandal. Nevertheless, Nelson's obsession about the Prince of Wales gave rise to numerous long, hysterical letters. Rationality only returned when, having changed ship to the *St George*, in readiness for the Baltic expedition, he was allowed three day's leave, in which he rushed to London.

Throughout these events Sir William behaved with complete discretion. Not only did he turn a blind eye to his wife's birth of a child but even wrote to reassure Nelson when Emma was 'indisposed' from digestive troubles. Ironically, his understanding attitude only permitted passions between Nelson and Emma to intensify.

After Nelson's visit to London the pain of departure was renewed once more.

Parting from such a friend is literally tearing one's own flesh; but the remembrance will keep up our spirits till we meet. My affection is, if possible, stronger than ever for you, and I trust it will keep increasing as long as we both live. I have seen Mrs Thomson's friend, who is delighted at my having seen his dear child ...

The visit had given Nelson a new level of confidence in his relationships with both Emma and Fanny. On 1 March he wrote to Emma:

Now, my own dear wife, for such you are in my eyes and in the face of heaven, I can give full scope to my feelings, for I daresay Oliver will faithfully deliver this letter. You know, my dearest Emma, that there is nothing in this world that I would not do for us to live together, and to have our dear little child with us ...

Three days later he wrote to Fanny. He had, he maintained, done all he could for his stepson, Josiah, who would receive command of another ship:

> I have done my duty as an honest generous man and I neither want or wish for any body to care what become of me, whether I return or am left in the Baltic, seeing I have done all in my power for you. And if dead you will find I have done the same, therefore my only wish is to be left to myself and wishing you every happiness, believe that I am your affectionate Nelson and Brontë.

It was what Fanny termed 'my Lord Nelson's letter of dismissal'. She wrote to him, repeatedly assuring him of her affection, and in December she appealed to him for the last time. 'Do, my dear husband, let us live together.' But the letter was returned to Fanny with a note by Alexander Davison that stated, 'Opened by mistake by Lord Nelson, but not read'.

Settled in his own mind, Nelson turned his attention to professional matters. In March he sailed for the Baltic under the command of Admiral Sir Hyde Parker. They were to force the Danes to withdraw from the 'Neutrality of the North', formed by the Baltic states to deter the Royal Navy from interfering with their trade with France. If the Danes resisted, Parker was to destroy their fleet, which had the power of closing the Sound – the only really navigable passage into the Baltic – to British shipping carrying naval stores vital to the Navy's capability to wage war at sea. The Danes had over 20 ships

LEFT: Sir Hyde Parker, commander-in-chief in the Baltic at the time of the Battle of Copenhagen; 'a good-tempered man, full of vanity, a great deal of pomp, and a pretty smattering of ignorance'.

RIGHT: *Danish print of the Battle of Copenhagen. 'Here was no manoevring,' Nelson was to record. 'It was downright fighting.'*

of the line; the British fleet consisted of 15 ships of similar power, with two 50-gun ships and some brigs, bomb vessels and frigates.

Near Copenhagen Parker expressed a desire to impose British terms by enforcing a blockade on the Baltic. However, this would allow the Baltic powers time to concentrate their naval forces. Nelson therefore recommended that Copenhagen and the Danish fleet, anchored in defensive formation in the King's Deep in front of the city, should be attacked immediately. Parker was persuaded by Nelson's argument, and Nelson took ten ships of the line south past the city along a wide, deep eastern channel, before turning north to close in and attack. He himself transferred to the 74-gun *Elephant*, which had a shallower draft than the *St George*. This remained north of the city with the other largest ships under Parker's command.

The attack took place as a cold, calculating blow, when the wind turned favourable from the south on 2 April 1801. Two hours after the conflict began,

on seeing two British ships fly distress signals and one appear to ground, Parker made the signal to leave off the action, primarily to give Nelson latitude to withdraw should he want to. Piqued and angry, Nelson put a telescope to his blind eye and, with characteristic bravado, exclaimed to the *Elephant's* captain, 'You know, Foley, I have only one eye – I have the right to be blind sometimes. I really do not see the signal.'

The Danes continued defiant, in spite of great damage to their anchored ships. After three hours Nelson sent an ultimatum: 'If the firing is continued on the part of Denmark, Lord Nelson will be obliged to set on fire all the floating batteries he has taken without having the power of saving the brave Danes who have defended them.' A ceasefire followed, Nelson going on shore next morning

LEFT: *British view of the line-up of ships at the Battle of Copenhagen, the Danish fleet anchored inshore. Nelson was put in command of the battle, which he fought from the* Elephant. *'It is warm work, and this day may be the last to us at any moment', he was heard to remark as the mainmast was hit by fire. 'But mark you, I would not be anywhere else for thousands.'*

BELOW: *Plate from a Coalport dinner service decorated with Nelson's full coat of arms within an oak-leaf border.*

to negotiate an extension to the truce. Later it was extended into a 14-week armistice, Nelson again conducting British diplomacy, and the whole 'Armed Neutrality' collapsed when news was received that one of its prime movers, Tsar Paul I of Russia, had been assassinated.

When news of the Battle of Copenhagen reached London, with copies of all the correspondence that had passed between Nelson and Parker, the latter was recalled on account of his inactivity and timidity, while Nelson succeeded to his command. In May he paraded the British fleet off Revel and Kronstadt, the Swedish and Russian naval bases, further contributing to the dissolution of the Armed Neutrality. In mid-June, once more off Copenhagen, he received news that he had been created a viscount and relieved of his command. He landed at Great Yarmouth on 1 July 1801, first visiting casualties in hospital, then hastening to London.

With St Vincent now First Lord of the Admiralty, and Britain threatened by invasion from France, Nelson had little time to be with Emma and Horatia. He spent a few days in Surrey and the Thames Valley, staying at inns with Sir William and Emma. On 20 July he was summoned to the Admiralty and on 26 July received an appointment to command a counter-invasionary force that was gathered to defend the Thames and Medway rivers, and the coastlines of Kent, Sussex and Essex between Beachy Head and Orford Ness.

With typical enthusiasm, when action was called for, he threw himself into the new command, which he managed from Deal, in Kent. Emma, he hoped, might come and stay nearby on shore. Considering attack was the best form of defence, he proposed a raid on the flotilla of French invasion barges moored at Boulogne, an operation he planned for the night of 15 August. That evening he wrote to Emma:

BELOW: *Plate from the same service decorated with an anchor and laurel wreath, and commemorating the Baltic campaign.*

RIGHT: *French print of Nelson's bombardment of the invasion flotilla gathered at Boulogne on 5 August 1801 prior to the British attack of 15 August.*

From my heart I wish you could find me out a good comfortable house, I should hope to be able to purchase it. At this moment I can command only £3,000; as to asking Sir William, I could not do it; I would sooner beg.

Turning to the forthcoming action, he continued:

As you may believe, my dear Emma, my mind feels at which is going forward this night; it is one thing to order and arrange an attack and another to execute it. But, I assure you, I have taken much more precaution for others, than if I was to go myself ... After they have fired their guns, if one half of the French do not jump overboard and swim on shore, I will venture to be hanged ... If our people behave as I expect, our loss cannot be much. My fingers itch to be at them.

The attack that night was a tragic failure. The French had expected it and moored their ships across the harbour mouth with chain cables. They were protected from boarding with nets and manned with soldiers as well as seamen, armed with muskets and grapeshot. As at Tenerife, a current bore the attacking boats past their targets. From the British boats, 45 men were killed and 128 wounded. Among the wounded were two friends, Captain Edward Parker and Lieutenant Frederick Langford, for whom Nelson rented rooms in Deal for them to recover. Returning from a visit to Parker, he wrote to Emma:

I come on board, but no Emma. No, no, my heart will break. I am in silent distraction. My dearest wife, how can I bear our separation? Good God! What a change. I am so low that I cannot hold up my head.

Parker was to die, and Nelson 'grieved almost to death', weeping openly at his funeral. That summer and autumn Nelson was frequently depressed. The Hamiltons came to visit him for a while, staying at Deal. But without his friends, and especially Emma, close by to comfort him, he found life full of 'sorrow and sadness'. Moreover, the Admiralty declined to grant him leave, even for reasons of ill health. For this he particularly blamed Troubridge, his old subordinate and now one of St Vincent's Admiralty commissioners. Even Hardy, appointed his flag captain, noticed that the Admiralty opposed him in everything, apparently wishing 'to clip his wings a little'. Relief came only in September when Emma announced that she had found him a house, at Merton in Surrey. He brightened immediately:

You may rely upon one thing, that I shall like Merton; therefore do not be uneasy on that account. I have that opinion of your taste and judgement that I do not believe it can fail in pleasing me. We must only consider our means;

and, for the rest, I am sure, you will soon make it the prettiest place in the world ... If I can afford to buy the duck close and the field adjoining, it would be pleasant; but I shall know when my accounts are settled at New Year's Day. To be sure we shall employ the trades-people of our village in preference to any others, in what we want for common use, and give them every encouragement to be kind and attentive to us.

Turning his thoughts to Horatia, he continued:

Whatever, my dear Emma, you do for my little charge, I must be pleased with. Probably, she will be lodged at Merton; at least, in the spring, when she can have the benefit of our walks. It will make the poor mother happy, I am sure. I do not write to her to-day, as this goes through the Admiralty; but, tell her all I would say. You know my unchangeable thoughts about her. I shall have the child christened when I come up. Have we a nice church at Merton? We will set an example of goodness to the underparishioners.

The surveyor's report on Merton Place was damning, but both Nelson and Emma were set on it. Sir William, too, was quickly taken by it. Soon after moving in, he wrote to Nelson:

I have lived with our dear Emma some several years. I know her merits, have an opinion of the head & heart that God Almighty has been pleased to give her; but a seaman alone could have given a fine woman full power to chuse and fit up a residence for him without seeing it himself ... You have nothing but to come and enjoy it immediately. You have a good mile of pleasant dry walk around your farm. It would make you laugh to see Emma & her mother fitting up pig-sties and hen-coops, and already the canal is enlivened with ducks and the cock is strutting with his hens along the walks ...

That October 1801, when negotiations for peace with France began, Nelson saw his new home for the first time. He was delighted. Allowed a free hand,

ABOVE: *Miniature of Emma's mother, known as Mrs Cadogan. She accompanied Emma to Naples and was ever-present in the background of Emma's life. Later, she was a frequent visitor to Merton Place.*

ABOVE: *Needlework picture by Emma representing her and Nelson at Merton. 'You are in luck,' Sir William wrote, 'for, on my conscience I verily believe that a place so suitable to your views could not have been found.'*

RIGHT: *Portico of Merton Place, a page from a sketchbook of Thomas Baxter, 1802. Nelson first saw the house in October 1801 and was delighted, exclaiming, 'Is this, too, mine', as he saw the house and garden, and the small farmyard.*

Emma cultivated domesticity with a peculiar gift. As she was unable to keep Horatia there, she mothered Charlotte, Nelson's niece. Charlotte enjoyed the walks, games, fishing with Sir William and having singing lessons with Emma.

Soon, under Emma's influence, the house came to resemble a shrine to Nelson's fame and victories, a physical manifestation of the manner in which she treated Nelson. One who was appalled by what he saw was Lord Minto, the diplomat, an old professional friend of Nelson, who visited Merton early in 1802. He reported indignantly to his wife:

ABOVE: *Emma and Charlotte, Nelson's niece. Charlotte was a regular and happy guest at Merton Place, and very attentive to Nelson.*

The whole establishment and way of life is such as to make me angry, as well as melancholy; but I cannot alter it, and I do not think myself obliged or at liberty to quarrel with him for his weakness, though nothing shall ever induce me to give the smallest countenance to Lady Hamilton. She looks ultimately to the chance of marriage, as Sir W. will not be long in her way, and she probably indulges a hope that she may survive Lady Nelson; in the meanwhile she and Sir William and the whole set of them are living with him at his expense. She is in high looks, but more immense than ever. She goes on cramming Nelson with trowelfuls of flattery, which he goes on taking as quietly as a child does pap. The love she makes to him is not only ridiculous, but disgusting: not only the rooms, but the whole house, staircases and all, are covered with nothing but pictures of her and him, of all sizes and sorts, and representations of his naval actions, coats of arms, pieces of plate in his honour, the flagstaff of 'L'Orient' etc. – an excess of vanity which counteracts its own purpose. If it was Lady H.'s house there might be a pretence

for it; to make his own a mere looking-glass to view himself all day is bad taste.

It was a household within which even Sir William's diplomacy was sorely tested. In January 1802 he admitted to his nephew, Charles Greville, that he thought it:

> but reasonable after having fagged all my life that my last days should pass off comfortably and quietly. Nothing at present disturbs me but my debt & the nonsense I am obliged to submit to here, to avoid coming to an explosion, which would be attended with many disagreeable effects & would totally destroy the comfort of the best man and best friend I have in the world. However I am determined that my quiet shall not be disturbed, let the nonsensical world go as it will.

His relationship with Emma steadily deteriorated to a point in 1802 when he could only communicate by letter his desire for a quieter life. He wrote to her:

> I have no complaint to make but I feel the whole attention of my wife is given to Ld N. and his interest at Merton. I well know the purity of Ld N.'s friendship for Emma and me, and I know how very uncomfortable it would make his Lp, our best friend, if a separation should take place, & am therefore determined to do all in my power to prevent such an extremity, which would be essentially detrimental to all parties, but would be more sensibly felt by our dear friend than by us.

Determined 'not to have more of the very silly altercations that happen but too often between us and embitter the present moments exceedingly', he urged that they should 'bear and forbear for God's sake'.

Such a policy of deliberate tolerance on Sir William's part gave Nelson the settled domestic life he had always craved.

LEFT: *Playing at cards, Emma's head framed by the arms of the candelabrum. These two intimate drawings of life at Merton are by Baxter, whom Nelson met on his tour of the West Country.*

BELOW: *Gillray's caricature of 'A Cognoscenti Contemplating the Beauties of the Antique' shows the aged Sir William peering with his usual interest at a collection of antiquities and failing to see that most of them satirize him as a cuckolded husband.*

HORATIA

ORATIA WAS BORN to Emma Hamilton on 29 or 30 January 1801 at the house rented by Sir William Hamilton at 23 Piccadilly, in London. As soon as she was able, Emma took her to be nursed by a Mrs Gibson in Little Titchfield Street.

Nelson had already invented the fiction of Mr and Mrs Thomson, a seaman serving with him, the wife with Emma, for whom they passed messages about their 'trying situation'. At the birth of the child the seaman went 'mad with joy'.

Separated from events in London, on board the *San Josef*, Nelson expended his energies in planning and providing for Horatia's financial security. He was particularly conscious of the need to shield her from the 'disgrace' of illegitimacy. He thus drew up a memorandum bequeathing all his surplus money above the first £20,000 to Horatia, with Emma acting as guardian, to maintain and educate 'this female child' as his own. Three years later he made Horatia a further bequest of £4,000.

Nelson saw his daughter for the first time on his visit to London on 24 to 25 February 1801. She was, so Nelson thought, like Emma in the upper part of her face. His letters to Emma thereafter repeatedly thanked her for caring for his child, as though he was conscious that Horatia meant far more to him than she did to Emma. After Nelson took up residence at Merton Place in October 1801, Horatia was brought there whenever Sir William was absent.

Horatia was christened before Nelson's departure to join the Mediterranean fleet in May 1803, a month after Sir William's death. Emma was again pregnant, and Nelson was unable to persuade her to establish Horatia at Merton. Instead, Emma left her with Mrs Gibson and saw her even less than before. She had failed to have Horatia

innoculated against smallpox, to which Nelson was favourable, and Horatia became ill with it early in 1804. In May 1805 Nelson took it upon himself to terminate Mrs Gibson's care of his daughter. But Horatia was still not moved to Merton until August, when Nelson returned home for the last time.

Horatia, then aged four and a half, later recalled Nelson's presence there with affection. But naturally she did not remember

LEFT: *Nelson began to write to Horatia when she was two, receiving replies written on Horatia's behalf by Emma. Nelson sent her the gold necklace with a dog pendant in response to her request for a dog. The miniature of Horatia is by James Holmes.*

RIGHT: *Horatia with a tambourine, echoing a painting of Emma by Madame Vigée-Lebrun. 'Kiss dear Horatia a thousand times for me', Nelson wrote from the Victory.*

Nelson's repeated returns to her room on the night of his departure for the *Victory*, on the last to kneel by her bed and pray for her blessing. As ever, Nelson wrote from sea that his heart and soul remained with Emma and Horatia.

Following the news of Nelson's death, Emma moved to Clarges Street, where she mourned and received visitors and, once Nelson's codicils to his will were published in the newspapers, fended off polite enquiries as to the origin of Miss Horatia Nelson Thomson. Nelson's relatives, however, had no need to wonder, and in 1806 Emma and Horatia together were invited to visit the Boltons at Burnham Market in Norfolk and the Matchams at Horsham in Sussex.

Horatia was taken to the heart of these families, the sacred relic of the man whom they loved. Only Nelson's brother William, who succeeded as Viscount Nelson (and was created an earl in honour of the deceased) and received the main financial rewards from the Government, remained suspicious and distant.

After Merton Place was sold, Horatia accompanied Emma on a succession of moves from one London residence to another. Emma invented the story that Horatia's mother was Queen of the Two Sicilies at Naples, and Horatia naturally came to wonder who her mother was. Arrested for debt in 1813 and later released, Emma crossed to France with Horatia to avoid her creditors in 1814. They lived in a single room in Calais, where, with Horatia attending on her, Emma died in January 1815.

That same month Horatia turned 14. She returned to England to live with the Matchams, then the Boltons. In 1822 she married a curate named Philip Ward, and their first son was named Horatio Nelson. Between 1844 and 1846 she co-operated with Sir Harris Nicolas in the seven-volume publication of Nelson's letters. She never came to acknowledge that Lady Hamilton was her mother. She died on 6 March 1881.

He was able to entertain his father at Merton, a visit that went well in spite of the latter's sympathies with Fanny. Edmund Nelson died in April 1802. Nelson did not attend the funeral at Burnham Thorpe for fear of meeting his wife, but everyone at Merton went into deep mourning.

In the same year he attended the Lord Mayor's Show and had the horses of his coach removed and was drawn through the streets to the Guildhall by the London crowd. Charlotte was there and marvelled at 'all the people jumping up to the carriage' to see her uncle, and 'thousands of people round him looking at him ... all the ladies had their handkerchiefs out of the windows when my uncle passed, they and the people calling out Nelson for ever'.

BELOW: John Downman's portrait of 1802, inscribed 'Admiral Lord Nelson of the Nile, Who conquer'd foe with wondrous spoil'. Edmund Nelson on his last visit to Merton found his son 'in better health and happier in himself' than he had ever seen him.

Early in the summer of 1802 Nelson accompanied the Hamiltons on a tour of the West Country and South Wales to inspect Sir William's estates. They were snubbed by the Duke of Marlborough at Blenheim Palace, near Oxford, but otherwise welcomed by cathedral bells, parades of yeomanry, musical bands and cheering crowds wherever they went: Gloucester, Ross, Monmouth, Abergavenny, Brecon, Carmarthen, Milford Haven, Tenby, Chepstow, Monmouth again, Hereford, Ludlow, Worcester, Birmingham and back to Merton. The jubilation with which they were received was observed by a nine-year-old, William Macready, in the theatre at Birmingham:

> When ... he entered his box, the uproar of the
> house was deafening and it seemed as if it would
> know no end ... Lady Hamilton laughing loud and
> without stint, clapped with uplifted hands and with all
> her heart and kicked her heels against the footboard of the

seat, while Nelson placidly and with his mournful look ... bowed repeatedly to the oft-repeated cheers.

Otherwise the trio remained at Merton. Then, on 6 April 1803, Sir William died. Emma held him in her arms, while Nelson held his hand. Emma's desperate distress was judged by some to be theatrical, but there had been deep affection and understanding between the two. To maintain proprieties, Nelson immediately vacated Merton for lodgings in Piccadilly.

There was much to engross him in London. War was brewing once more, and on 14 May he received an appointment from the Admiralty. Before leaving London he accompanied Emma to Marylebone church where Horatia, now two, was christened 'Horatia Nelson Thompson [*sic*]'. He then departed for the *Victory* at Portsmouth. The domestic idyll was over, but the peace and comfort had renewed his strength. At midday on 20 May 1803, after going on board, he wrote to Emma:

> You will believe that although I am glad to leave that horrid
> place, Portsmouth, yet the being afloat makes me now feel
> that we do not tread the same element. I feel from my soul
> God is good, and in His due wisdom will unite us, only
> when you look upon our dear child call to your
> remembrance all you think that I would say was I present,
> and be assured that I am thinking of you every moment. My
> heart is full to bursting! May God Almighty bless & protect
> you, is the fervent prayer of, my dear beloved Emma, your
> most faithful, affectionate Nelson & Brontë.

RIGHT: *'You, my beloved Emma, and my country, are the two dearest objects of my fond heart – a heart susceptible and true.' The drawing of Emma is by Baxter.*

CHAPTER EIGHT

TRAFALGAR

NELSON HAD BEEN GIVEN COMMAND of the Mediterranean, like Lord St Vincent and Lord Keith before him. He was required to leave the *Victory* off Ushant Island, near Brittany, with Admiral Cornwallis should Cornwallis need it, and to transfer his flag to the frigate *Amphion* to continue his voyage to Toulon via Malta and Naples. After crossing the Channel, on 22 May he wrote a farewell letter to Emma:

> We are now in sight of Ushant, and shall see Admiral Cornwallis in an hour. I am not in a little fret on the idea that he may keep the *Victory*, and turn us all into the *Amphion*. It will make it truly uncomfortable; but I cannot help myself. I assure you, my dear Emma, that I feel a thorough conviction that we shall meet again, with honour, riches, and health, and remain together till a good old age. I look at your and my God's Child's picture; but, till I am sure of remaining here, I cannot bring myself to hang them up. Be assured that my attachment and affectionate regard is unalterable; nothing can shake it! And, pray, say so to my dear Mrs T. when you see her. Tell her, that my love is unbounded, to her and her dear sweet; and, if she should have more, it will extend to all of them. In short, my dear Emma, say everything to her which your dear, affectionate heart and head can think of.

His task was to defend Gibraltar, Malta and the Kingdom of the Two Sicilies; to watch the French fleet in Toulon, and to destroy it should it venture forth; most importantly, to prevent the Toulon fleet reaching and joining with the French fleet from Brest, for Napoleon's army of invasion was poised around Boulogne waiting for the French navy to gain command of the English Channel. To carry out these

RIGHT: *The* Victory, *ordered in 1758, the year that Nelson was born, and launched in 1765. Preparing to set sail in her from Portsmouth in 1803, Nelson wrote to Captain Sutton, 'If you can get twelve good sheep, some hay, and fowls and corn, it will do no harm.'*

RIGHT: *Scene in a midshipmen's berth. During the blockade of Toulon the sailors spent many months at sea without setting foot on land, diverting themselves in any way they could find. Nelson himself was irked by the monotony of waiting for the French to come out of harbour: 'We cruise, cruise, and one day so much like another that they are scarcely distinguishable.'*

duties, after the *Victory* rejoined him in July 1803, he had ten ships of the line and three frigates. One battleship had to watch Cadiz, in case the Spanish were persuaded again to ally themselves with France. Another had to stay close to Naples, while one or two of the remainder took it in turns to patrol the local coastlines, looking into ports and fetching fresh water, live cattle and sheep, onions and oranges, from friendly markets to keep the fleet free from scurvy.

Blockade duty on fine days could be pleasant, but at all times of year the Gulf of Lyons had regular gales and heavy swells. In late September he observed to Emma:

> We have had, for these fourteen days past, nothing but gales of wind and a heavy sea. However, as our ships have suffered no damage, I hope to be able to keep the sea all the winter. Nothing but dire necessity shall force me to that out of the way place, Malta. If I had depended upon that island ... our ships' companies would have been done for long ago. However, by management, I have got supplies from Spain, and also from France; but it appears that we are almost shut out from Spain, for they begin to be very uncivil to our ships.

Ships that went for fresh food and supplies often lost men from desertion. To counter the problem Nelson initially appealed to the loyalty of his crews but

made clear he was ready to punish offenders with the full force of naval discipline. A general memorandum to the seamen of the fleet sent out in November 1803 reads:

> Lord Nelson is very sorry to find that notwithstanding his forgiveness of the men who deserted in Spain, it has failed to have its proper effect, and that there are still men who so far forget their duty to their King and country as to desert at a time when every man in England is in arms to defend it against the French. Therefore Lord Nelson desires that it may be perfectly understood that if any man be so infamous as to desert from the service in future, he will not only be brought to a court-martial, but that if the sentence should be death, it will be most assuredly carried into execution.

BELOW: *In the Gulf of Lyons, Nelson ran into bad weather, and for two weeks the ships would have sailed close-reefed, as in Darcy Lever's illustration.*

Nelson's main problem was not morale, or scurvy, but the state of his ships. After a war lasting eight years, and little more than a year of peace, the British navy was in poor condition. In the rush to gain command of the sea, the dockyards had equipped them quickly with whatever rigging they had in store. The consequence was that most ships had to be re-rigged at sea by artificers in the fleet; for at the beginning of the Napoleonic War there was no local naval base east of Gibraltar. Indeed, owing to the extent of French power not even Leghorn was available, so that Nelson had to use the bleak Maddalena Islands off the north coast of Sardinia for his land base.

Life in command of the fleet suited Nelson and, after growing accustomed to absence from Emma, his spirits remained buoyant. In a letter to the British ambassador to Naples, Hugh Elliot, on 1 November 1803 he wrote:

> The fleet being very much in want of water, I have taken the opportunity of the moonlight nights to come here [Maddalena Islands] in order to obtain it, and some

refreshments for our crews, who have now been upwards of five months at sea. But our health and good humour is perfection, and we only want the French fleet out. This day week they had eight sail of the line ready, and a ninth fitting; so that we shall surely meet them some happy day, and I have no doubt but that we shall be amply repaid for all our cares and watchings.

Once life at sea had settled into a routine, with exercise, letter-writing and dinner with his officers, the Mediterranean winter passed relatively calmly for him. Distant from England and Emma, and free from both ambition and anger, he acquired an emotional stability that had long been lacking. Indeed, he sensibly deterred Emma from trying to visit him in the Mediterranean, and instead encouraged her in caring for Horatia. He now wanted the child to live at Merton, though there he worried that she might fall into the garden's canal-like pond, which they called 'the Nile'. He thought about providing for his daughter's financial independence, he sent her presents and, as she grew older, wrote her letters. The first he sent on 21 October 1803, two years to the day before he died, and it conveyed his constant preoccupation with that possibility.

My dear Child, Receive this first letter from your most affectionate Father. If I live, it will be my pride to see you virtuously brought up; but if it pleases God to call me, I trust to Himself: in that case, I have left Lady H. your guardian. I therefore charge you, my Child, on the value of a Father's blessing, to be obedient and attentive to all her kind admonitions and instructions. At this moment I have left you, in a Codicil dated the 6th of September, the sum of four thousand pounds sterling, the interest of which is to be paid to your guardian for your maintenance and education. I shall only say,

BELOW: *'Your goodness of heart, your amiable qualities, your unbounded charity will make you envied in the world which is to come,' Nelson wrote to Emma. The letter ends, 'God's will be done. Amen, amen.'*

my dear Child, may God Almighty bless you and make you an ornament to your sex, which I am sure you will be if you attend to all Lady H's kind instructions; and be assured that I am, my dear Horatia, your most affectionate Father, Nelson & Brontë.

Presumably with Emma taking dictation, a correspondence ensued. A later letter from Nelson read:

LEFT: *Horatia at Merton Place by Baxter. After Sir William's death she lived at Merton whenever Nelson came home from sea.*

My dear Horatia, I feel much pleased by your kind letter and for your present of a lock of your beautiful hair. I am very glad to hear that you are so good and mind everything which your governess Miss Connor and dear Lady Hamilton tell you. I send you a lock of my hair and a pound note to buy a locket to put it in and I give you leave to wear it when you are dressed and behave well, and I send you another to buy some little thing for Mary and your governess. I am sure that for the world you would not tell a story. It must have slipt my memory that I promised you a Watch, therefore I have sent to Naples to get one and I will send it home as soon as it arrives – the Dog I never could have promised as we have no Dogs on board ship. Only I beg my dear Horatia be obedient and you will ever be sure of the affection of Nelson & Brontë.

The calm was disrupted early in 1804, when Horatia caught smallpox and Emma entered the final stages of another pregnancy. Nelson was kept on tenterhooks, writing on 2 April:

I have, my dearest beloved Emma, been so uneasy for this last month; desiring most ardently to hear of your well doing! Captain Capel brought me your letters, sent by the Thisbe, from Gibraltar. I opened – opened – found none but December, and early in January. I was in such an agitation! At last, I found one without a date: which, thank God! told my poor heart that you was recovering; but that dear little Emma was no more! and, that Horatia had been so very ill – it all together upset me. But it was just at bed-time; and I had time to reflect, and be thankful to God for sparing you and our dear Horatia. I am sure, the loss of one – much more, both – would have drove me mad. I was so agitated, as it was, that I was glad it was night, and that I could be by myself. Kiss dear Horatia for me: and tell her to be a dutiful and good child; and, if she is, that we shall always love her.

When he had transferred back into the *Victory*, he was pleased to take Captain Thomas Hardy with him as his flag-captain. The two worked well together and, though Nelson occasionally took it into his head to interfere with the sailing of the ship, he was normally able to leave its whole management to Hardy. In his own work he was helped by the multi-lingual chaplain, Alexander Scott, who translated foreign newspapers taken from prizes and read aloud to him.

Nelson's habit of exercising on deck in all weathers, without taking pains to protect or properly dry himself, affected his health and, in May 1804, he observed to Dr Baird at the Sick and Wounded Board in London:

> The health of this fleet cannot be exceeded; I really believe that my shattered carcase is in the worst plight of the whole fleet. I have had a sort of rheumatic fever, they tell me; but I have felt the blood gushing up the left side of my head, and the moment it covers the brain, I am fast asleep. I am now better of that; and with violent pain in my side, and night sweats, with heat in the evening, and quite flushed. The pain in my heart, nor spasms, I have not had for some time. Mr Magrath, whom I admire for his great abilities every day I live, gives me excellent remedies ...

The remedies included camphor and opium, but even these could not stave off what seem to have been symptoms of stress. Nelson continued:

> The constant anxiety I have experienced has shook my weak frame and my rings will hardly keep upon my fingers. What gives me more [concern than anything] is that I can every month perceive a visible (if I may be allowed the

ABOVE: *The cartoon shows Nelson dragging his enemy prizes to the feet of Britannia. Napoleon, standing on the left, declares, 'I want not your Forts, your Cities and your Territories, Sir, I only want Ships, Colonies and Commerce'.*

expression) loss of sight. A few years must, as I have always predicted, render me blind. I have often heard that blind people are cheerful, but I think I shall take it to heart.

He was better by June but, as the Mediterranean summer moved into winter, he began to appeal for leave for a rest. He was looking forward to spending Christmas at Merton.

Then, in December, Spain entered the war on the side of France, and the danger increased of their fleets combining to overwhelm the British navy in the Channel. On a stormy night in mid-January 1805 the whole French fleet escaped from Toulon. The French squadron in Rochefort had escaped two weeks earlier, and there were fears that the French invasion plan was at last being put into operation.

In desperation, and reminiscent of his search before the Battle of the Nile, Nelson plunged back into the eastern Mediterranean, looking into Naples, Palermo, Malta and Alexandria. Returning to Malta, he learned that the storms that had momentarily lifted the British blockade of Toulon had damaged and driven the escaping French back in again almost immediately.

However the enemy had not given up their plan. On 30 March, while off Majorca, Nelson heard that the French had emerged again, though their whereabouts was unknown. Falling back on the island of Ustica, north of Palermo, to gather more information, Nelson heard on 18 April that the Toulon fleet had passed through the Straits of Gibraltar some ten days earlier. Opposed by contrary winds, it was nearly a month later that his own fleet was able to follow them. Off Cape Trafalgar in early May, he received information that the French had picked up some Spanish vessels from Cadiz and had been sighted heading for the West Indies. Thirty-one days behind, Nelson sailed in chase of them.

At Barbados on 4 June he was informed by General Robert Brereton, commanding on St Lucia, that 28 enemy vessels had been sighted sailing south. Later he was to blame Brereton for misinforming him; for at Grenada on 9 June

ABOVE: *Thomas Masterman Hardy, pictured in about 1801. 'By God, I'll not lose Hardy' were Nelson's words when as a lieutenant Hardy had been in danger of capture. He became Nelson's trusted friend and his longest-serving flag-captain.*

he learned that the enemy had passed Dominica and Antigua heading north and that they had taken a convoy of British sugar ships. He concluded that they must be returning to Europe, and subsequent reports confirmed the belief. Sending a frigate ahead in warning, Nelson again set sail in pursuit.

A month later, on 18 July, without having had any sight of the enemy, he encountered Collingwood's squadron off Cadiz and put into Gibraltar. Shortly afterwards, off Cape Finisterre on 22 July, Sir John Calder's squadron intercepted the Franco-Spanish fleet and fought an inconclusive skirmish. On 28 July the enemy put into Vigo, then on 1 August slipped into Ferrol, further north. Later they again moved south, to Cadiz. Napoleon's plan to have the Combined Fleet join with the Brest fleet and invade the Channel had been blocked.

Nelson was mortified at his failure to find and destroy the enemy in the West Indies. When he went ashore at Gibraltar, it was the first time he had set foot off the *Victory* for almost two years, and most seamen in the fleet had been at sea for as long. They had pursued the enemy with a spirit that threatened it with destruction, and one that was essential to the maintenance of morale in England. For, with Napoleon's army still camped along the French coast, the Combined Fleet of the enemy at liberty still posed the threat of imminent invasion.

At Gibraltar Nelson was given leave and he sailed for Portsmouth in the *Victory*. He reached Merton early on 22 August, to a house crowded with relatives. Horatia, now four and a half, delighted him. Emma thrilled him as much as ever, and outside, wherever he went, he drew admirers.

An American, Benjamin Silliman, spotted him in the Strand, in London, on 26 August:

> He was walking, in company with his chaplain, and as usual followed by a crowd ... Lord Nelson cannot appear in the

RIGHT: *Cuthbert, Lord Collingwood, Vice-Admiral of the Red. Of his friendship with Nelson he wrote, 'Since the year 1773 we have been on terms of the greatest intimacy. Chance has thrown us very much together in service, and on many occasions we have acted in concert.'*

streets without immediately collecting a retinue, which augments as he proceeds, and when he enters a shop the door is thronged till he comes out, when the air rings with huzzas, and the dark cloud of the populace again moves on, and hangs upon his skirts.

Lord Minto met Nelson the same day 'in a mob in Piccadilly and got hold of his arm' so that he was mobbed too. Minto was moved 'to see the wonder and admiration, and love and respect, of the whole world; and genuine expression of all these sentiments at once, from gentle and simple, the moment he is seen'.

Minto went to dinner at Merton that night and found the family party sitting down to eat in the dining room, 'Lady Hamilton at the top of the table and Mother Cadogan [her mother] at the bottom'. He was impressed with the improvements Emma had made to the house while Nelson had been away – 'she is a clever being after all' – and commented on the lasting intensity of their relationship: 'the passion is as hot as ever'.

BELOW: *Baxter's watercolour of Merton Place. On 13 September 1805 Nelson wrote, 'at half past ten drove from dear Merton where I left all which [I] hold dear in this world to go and serve my King and Country.'*

Minto was with Nelson on 13 September, Nelson's last evening at Merton, after hearing that he was to have a fleet of 40 ships of the line, with frigates, sloops and smaller vessels, 'the largest command that any admiral has had for a long time'. He was to go to Portsmouth that night, and Emma, Minto afterwards recorded, was 'in tears all yesterday; could not eat, and hardly drink, and near swooning, and all at table'. Minto thought it 'a strange picture. She tells me nothing can be more pure and ardent than this flame. He is in many points a really great man, in others a baby.'

Nelson re-embarked on the *Victory* on Saturday evening, 14 September, being rowed off from 'the bathing machines' on the beach, instead of the usual place, to avoid the crowds. He was nevertheless surrounded by hundreds of people who cheered and to whom he responded by raising his hat. He arrived off Cadiz, where the Combined Fleet still sheltered, on 27 September and immediately took command of the British blockading fleet of 22 ships of the line from his old friend Cuthbert Collingwood. It pleased him that 'the officers

RIGHT: *Chart with the date 29 September 1805, showing the distinguishing 'Single and Double Pennants' to be flown by the various ships of the British fleet before the Battle of Trafalgar. It bears Nelson's signature.*

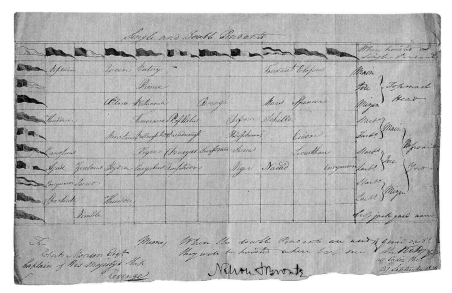

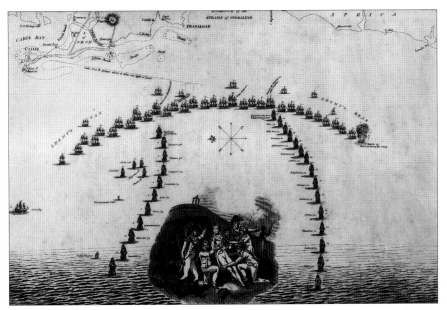

who came on board to welcome my return forgot my rank as Commander-in-Chief in the enthusiasm with which they greeted me'. It was two days before his forty-seventh birthday.

He immediately expressed his plan for attacking the enemy line when it emerged. He intended to divide his fleet into three divisions. Two of these, sailing in parallel columns, would cut the enemy line at right angles about one third of the way behind their leading ship and an equal distance from their rear. While their leading ships took time to go about, those at the centre and rear would be overwhelmed in a pell-mell battle. A reserve division, plus relatively undamaged ships, would then engage the enemy van when or if it turned to enter the battle. Not only was the plan 'generally approved, but clearly perceived and understood'.

The effort of resuming command and projecting his ideas undoubtedly took its toll. He wrote to Emma on 1 October:

NELSON'S TACTICS

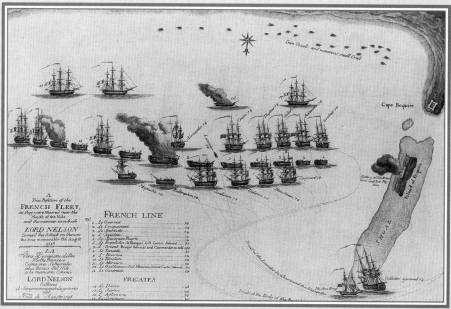

ROM THE FIRST Dutch War of 1652-4 to the 1790s the usual way of fighting a fleet engagement was for the opposing sides to form into two parallel lines of battle and engage broadside to broadside. Actions tended to be indecisive until Admiral Hawke used the tactic of a general chase to decimate a fleeing enemy when he drove the French fleet into Quiberon Bay in 1759 during the Seven Year's War.

At the Battle of the Saints in 1782, largely owing to a shift of wind, some of Admiral Rodney's ships passed through the French line and the resulting success included capture of their flagship. Later, at the Battle of the Glorious First of June 1794, Lord Howe ordered his ships to break through the French formation where possible and the result was a victorious mêlée in which six of the enemy ships were taken and one was sunk.

To Nelson, who had taken part in the chases of March and July 1795 in the Mediterranean, the superiority of British seamanship and gunnery were self-evident. He knew that these qualities would impose victory if only British ships were placed in point-blank proximity to their enemy. Banking on this superiority, and on the support of following captains, he deliberately turned his ship, the *Captain*, out of the British line at the Battle of Cape St Vincent early in 1797, to prevent two halves in the Franco-Spanish line from joining up. In so doing, he risked court-martial by Admiral Jervis for failing to keep as ordered to the line. However, his success in capturing two larger ships by boarding demonstrated to him the decisive value of precipitous mêlée tactics.

Consequently, Nelson had no doubts about the manner in which to attack the French fleet that he found in Aboukir Bay, Egypt, in 1798. While searching the Mediterranean for the French, he had discussed his ideas and plans with his captains and, on sighting the enemy, he had to make only one signal to guide them into battle.

The Battle of Copenhagen was less of a tactical victory than one where sheer nerve, determination and endurance counted above all else – qualities Nelson took for granted with British seamen.

Before the Battle of Trafalgar, Nelson's thinking aimed at precipitating a mêlée, leaving the completion of the victory to his captains and crews. Thus, 'the Nelson touch' was to launch his fleet in two parallel columns headlong into the enemy line about one-third and two-thirds of the way back from its leading ships. The greater part of the enemy fleet would then be overwhelmed before their leading ships could turn around to the aid of their centre and rear squadrons. Each of the different manoeuvres possible for the enemy to adopt was considered and in his mind countered. In the event, the mêlée involved most of the Franco-Spanish fleet.

Nelson, Collingwood wrote after Trafalgar, 'possessed the zeal of an enthusiast, directed by talents which nature had very bountifully bestowed upon him'; but the victory 'was the effect of system and nice combination, not of chance'.

LEFT: *'A true position of the French fleet, as they were moored near the Mouth of the Nile, and the manner in which Lord Nelson formed his attack on them on the eve of the ever memorable 1st of August 1798.'*

RIGHT: *'Lord Nelson Explaining to the Officers the Plan of Attack [at Trafalgar]'*, *an engraving published on the day of Nelson's funeral. At the briefing before the battle, 'Some shed tears, all approved – "It was new, it was singular, it was simple".'*

It is relief to me to take up the pen and write you a line; for I have had one of my dreadful spasms which has almost ennervated me ... The good people of England will not believe that rest of body and mind is necessary for me! But, perhaps, this spasm may not come again these six months. I have been writing seven hours yesterday; perhaps that had some hand in bringing it upon me ... I believe my arrival was most welcome; not only to the commander of the fleet, but also to every individual in it: and, when I came to explain to them the *Nelson touch*, it was like an electric shock. Some shed tears, all approved – 'It was new, it was singular, it was simple!' and, from admirals downwards, it was repeated – 'It must succeed, if ever they will allow us to get at them! You are, my Lord, surrounded by friends whom you inspire with confidence.' Some may be Judas's; but the majority are certainly much pleased with my commanding them.

Over the next three weeks the British fleet off Cadiz was increased to 27 ships of the line. On 14 October the enemy fleet was reported to have moved closer to the harbour mouth; on 19 October he knew the climactic moment was close:

My dearest, beloved Emma, the dear friend of my bosom, the signal has been made that the enemy's combined fleet are coming out of port. We have very little wind, so that I have no hopes of seeing them before tomorrow. May the God of Battles crown my endeavours with success; at all events, I will take care that my name shall ever be most dear to you and Horatia, both of whom I love as much as my own life; and as my last writing before the battle will be to you, so I hope in God that I shall live to finish my letter after the Battle. May heaven bless you prays your Nelson & Brontë.

Octr 20 in the morning we were close to the mouth of the Streights, but the wind had not come far enough to the westward to allow the combined fleets to weather the shoals of Trafalgar, but they were counted as far as forty

BELOW: *Letter written by Nelson to Henry Blackwood, captain of the* Euryalus. *'Truly we cannot miss getting hold of them and I will give them such a shaking as they never yet experienced,' he wrote of the coming confrontation, 'at least I will lay down my life in the attempt.'*

RIGHT: *Nelson's desk in the* Victory. *From here he wrote letters to Emma and Horatia, and a document leaving them as a legacy to his King and country.*

sail of ships of war, which I suppose to be 34 of the line and six frigates. A group of them was seen off the lighthouse off Cadiz this morning, but it blows so very fresh & thick weather that I rather believe they will go into the bay before night. May God Almighty give us success over these fellows, and enable us to get a peace.

As the Franco-Spanish fleet emerged and sailed south, Nelson kept his own out of sight over the horizon, sailing parallel 20 miles to the west. Next morning, 21 October, as the enemy followed the curve of the coastline south-east, he turned north-east and closed the distance between the fleets to ten miles, keeping the wind behind the British ships.

Retiring to his cabin, Nelson recorded the services Emma Hamilton had performed for the British Crown. As it was not in his power to reward her, he left:

Emma, Lady Hamilton, therefore a legacy to my King and country, that they will give her an ample provision to maintain her rank in

life. I also leave to the benefi-cence of my country, my adopted daughter, Horatia Nelson Thompson; and I desire she will use, in future, the name of Nelson only. These are the only favours I ask of the King and country, at this moment, when I am going to fight their battle. May God bless my King and country, and all those who I hold dear. My relations it is needless to mention, they will, of course, be amply provided for.

There were in fact 33 French and Spanish ships of the line, too many for the British fleet to be divided into three divisions. It thus formed into two columns, one led by

ABOVE: *Nelson's last letter to his 'Dearest beloved Emma, the dear friend of my bosom', written on 19 October 1805. His great affection for her was, as always, combined with the expression of his desire to serve his country.*

OPPOSITE PAGE: *The end of the Battle of Trafalgar, illustrating the scale of the action and of the destruction. The painting is by Nicholas Pocock.*

BELOW: *Coat worn by Nelson at the Battle of Trafalgar, with a hole in the left shoulder made by the fatal bullet. William Beatty, the ship's surgeon, warned that the wearing of decorations made him conspicuous to the enemy.*

Collingwood in the *Royal Sovereign*, the other led by Nelson in the *Victory*. About 11.00 a.m. the two leading ships were within three miles of the French and Spanish. With all furniture and other encumbrances cleared from the decks, Nelson returned to his chairless cabin and wrote kneeling at his desk:

> May the Great God, whom I worship, grant to my Country, and for the benefit of Europe in general, a great and glorious victory; and may no misconduct in any one tarnish it; and may humanity after Victory be the predominant feature in the British fleet. For myself, individually, I commit my life to Him who made me, and may the blessing light upon my endeavours for serving my Country faithfully. To Him I resign myself and the just cause which is entrusted to me to defend. Amen. Amen. Amen.

On deck once more, always thinking of the good conduct of his fleet, he sent the signal, 'England confides that every man will do his duty'. Time was short as the fleets closed, and instead of spelling out 'confides' in complicated hoists of flags, the word 'expects' was used, for which there was a single flag.

At midday the leading ships were a mile from the enemy line, which started to fire on them. Hardy, Nelson's secretary John Scott, and the surgeon William Beatty, became aware that Nelson was recognizable to snipers, having four chivalric decorations sewn on his admiral's coat. However, Nelson considered it was too late to change. As enemy fire became accurate, Scott was one of the first to be hit.

The British ships sailed head first into the broadsides of the French and Spanish. At 12.30 p.m. the *Victory* was able to choose her own opponent from three enemy vessels into which she was heading. Only then, as she steered into the smoke and flashing guns, was the ship able to open fire herself with crashing broadsides.

BELOW: *Pages from the log book of the* Euryalus *for 21 October 1805 on which is recorded Nelson's signal to the fleet, 'England expects that every man will do his duty'.*

Behind her and nearby, other British ships were pushing between French and Spanish vessels, breaking through their line, smashing its order and power, supporting one another to overwhelm and reduce each ship to surrender.

At 1.15 p.m. Nelson was hit by a sniper's musket shot from high on the mizzen mast of the French 74-gun *Redoubtable*. The ball entered his shoulder, passed through a lung and into his spine. He knew immediately his back was shot through and was carried, on Hardy's orders, down to the cockpit in the orlop deck below the waterline. On the way he gave orders to adjust the tiller ropes and placed a handkerchief over his face so that he would not be recognized. In the cockpit Beatty had him stripped of his clothes and examined him. Although he had no sensation in the lower part of his body, Nelson could feel the regular gushes of blood in his chest; his breathing was difficult and he had very severe pain at the point in the spine where the bullet had struck. Knowing he would not live long, he repeatedly told the chaplain in hurried, broken sentences:

> Remember me to Lady Hamilton! remember me to Horatia! remember me to all my friends. Doctor, remember me to Mr Rose [a senior politician and friend of Pitt, the Prime Minister]: tell him I have made a will, and left Lady Hamilton and Horatia to my Country.

But gradually he became calm enough to ask questions and enquire about the occasional cheering of the *Victory's* crew whenever an enemy ship was struck. He felt a strong thirst and called for drink and to be fanned with paper. Anxious for the safety of Hardy, he repeatedly sent messages requesting his attendance. Hardy came at last, an hour and ten minutes after Nelson had been brought down. They shook hands.

> I am a dead man, Hardy. I am going fast: it will be all over with soon. Come nearer to me. Pray let my dear Lady Hamilton have my hair, and all other things belonging to me.

After Hardy returned to the upper deck, Nelson told Beatty to attend to the other wounded, for all power and feeling below his chest had gone 'and you very well know I can live but a short time'. In the bustle around him, a wounded seaman waiting for amputation was hurt by someone passing by. Weak as he was, Nelson turned to the passer-by and reprimanded him for his 'lack of humanity'. The chaplain, Alexander Scott, attended to him. His pain was great and he kept repeating, 'God be praised, I have done my duty'.

Hardy came again an hour later. Once more they shook hands, Hardy holding on to Nelson's hand and congratulating him on a complete victory. To Hardy's question as to whether Collingwood would now take over the direction of affairs, Nelson replied, 'Not while I live, I hope, Hardy!' He attempted to raise himself and said, 'Take care of my dear Lady Hamilton, Hardy: take care of poor Lady Hamilton. Kiss me, Hardy.' Hardy then knelt and kissed his cheek. 'Now I am satisfied. Thank God, I have done my duty.' Hardy stood for a few minutes, knelt and again kissed Nelson's forehead. 'God bless you, Hardy!'

LEFT: The death of Nelson. The dying Admiral is supported by Captain Hardy, and in the group around him are Dr Beatty and a sailor bearing the ensign of a captured ship. This is a detail from an engraving after the painting by Daniel Maclise in the House of Lords. The artist studied existing portraits and interviewed survivors of the battle in the attempt to achieve authenticity.

Hardy departed. Nelson was turned on his side so as to breathe better, saying to the chaplain: 'Doctor, I have *not* been a *great* sinner'. He repeated his commitment of Emma and Horatia as a legacy to his country but his speech became fainter as the pain grew: 'drink, drink', 'fan, fan', 'rub, rub'. His last coherent words were the oft-repeated phrase, 'Thank God, I have done my duty.' He died at 4.30 p.m.

Of the ten ships in the enemy van, only five had been able to turn and enter the battle. Nelson's intention of overwhelming the rearward part of the enemy line had been completely successful. As the hours passed more French and Spanish vessels were reported to surrender, without any British losses. By the end of the day the combined Franco-Spanish fleet had lost 20 ships, with nearly 6,000 thousand men killed or wounded, and 20,000 seamen taken prisoner. The British lost 449 killed and 1,214 wounded. It was a devastating defeat for the combined powers, one from which their navies would only gradually recover and not before the end of the Napoleonic War ten years later. Temporarily, it put an end to threats of invasion and placed the British government once more on the offensive.

Nelson's death was mourned in the fleet and throughout Britain, nowhere more grievously than at Merton. There, Emma took to her bed. Receiving the last of his letters, she scrawled on it: 'Oh miserable, wretched Emma. Oh glorious & happy Nelson.' Neither she, nor Horatia, was to receive recognition as the legacy Nelson left to his country.

On receiving the news of Nelson's death, George III said simply, 'He died the death he wished'. Lord Castlereagh was more generous: 'Nelson has terminated his life in a manner worthy of himself.' Nelson's friend Lord Minto expressed what many contemporaries thought:

> One knows, on reflection, that such a death is the finest close, and the crown as it were, of such a life; and possibly, if his friends were angels and not men, they would acknowledge it as the last favour Providence could bestow and a seal and security for all the rest. His glory is certainly at its summit, and could be raised no higher by any length of life; but he might have lived at least to enjoy it.

He went on:

> We shall want more victories yet, and to whom can we look for them? The navy is certainly full of the bravest men, but ... brave as they almost all are, there was a sort of heroic cast about Nelson that I never saw in any other man, and which seems wanting to the achievement of *impossible things* which became easy to him, and on which the maintenance of our superiority at sea seems to depend against the growing navy of the enemy. However his example will do a great deal.

RIGHT: *Turner's impression of the scene on the deck of the* Victory, *where amid the smoke and confusion Nelson lay wounded. In the log book Hardy recorded, 'Partial firing continued until 4.30 pm when, a victory having been reported to the Right Hon. Lord Nelson K.B., Commander in Chief, he died of his wounds.'*

NELSON'S FUNERAL

AFTER TRAFALGAR, ON 22 OCTOBER 1805, Nelson's body was placed in a large cask that was filled with brandy. The cask was lashed to the *Victory's* mainmast and guarded by a sentry night and day. 'On the 24th there was a disengagement of air from the body to such a degree that the sentinel became alarmed on seeing the head of the cask raised'; the cask was spilled to allow the air to escape. On the voyage home the brandy was drained and replaced, legend claiming that the seamen sampled the drained spirits.

On the way from Spithead to the Nore, in the mouth of the Thames, an autopsy was performed. The fatal musket ball was removed, with gold-lace and material that clung to it from Nelson's epaulette and coat.

On 23 December Commissioner Grey's yacht met the *Victory* close to the Nore, and took the coffin, covered in an ensign, up the Thames to Greenwich. All the way up the river ships lowered their colours to half mast, bells were tolled and the forts at Tilbury and Gravesend fired minute guns. At Greenwich Hospital the coffin was placed in a private room until 4 January 1806, when it was displayed to the public in the Painted Hall for three days. Preceded by the Princess of Wales, nearly 100,000 people were said to have filed through the vast, heavily ornamented mourning chamber.

On 7 January a selected group of seamen from the *Victory* arrived at the Hospital, to be met by the Governor, Lord Hood. The following morning a procession assembled, the barges and boats stretching

LEFT: *Order of service at Nelson's funeral in St Paul's Cathedral on 9 January 1806. The service began at 1 pm. Thirty-two admirals and over a hundred captains attended. As they filed in with the coffin, seamen unfolded two Union Jacks and the ensign from the* Victory, *holed and torn by enemy shot.*

RIGHT: *Procession leaving Greenwich Hospital, where Nelson's coffin had lain in state in the Painted Hall. It was rowed up the Thames in a black-canopied barge to rest in the Admiralty overnight. The procession of boats on the river stretched for two miles.*

LEFT AND RIGHT: *The funeral barge and the car that bore Nelson's coffin from Whitehall to St Paul's. The decoration of the car was inspired by the head and stern of the* Victory.

almost two miles down the river to Woolwich. Kept back by lanes of armed Guards, Volunteers and Pikemen, local people were hurt as they pressed to get a view of the embarkation. Favoured by a flood tide, but against a hard south-westerly wind, the procession rowed up-river to reach Whitehall steps in two hours. There the body was processed to the Admiralty.

Early in the morning of 9 January 1806 the funeral procession assembled in Hyde Park, to which entry was limited by ticket. The marshalled coaches snaked across Piccadilly into St James's Park, through Horse Guards to the Admiralty. The procession moved off at midday, preceded by companies of light dragoons, infantry, cavalry, artillery and grenadiers. They were followed by pensioners from Greenwich Hospital, and seamen and marines of the *Victory*, walking in pairs in their ordinary clothes, black neck handkerchiefs and stockings, with crape in their hats. Naval officers, officials, ministers, noblemen and princes followed, the Prince of Wales last and nearest to the coffin. Family and close officers, including Captain Hardy, followed. At Temple Bar the procession was met by the Lord Mayor, aldermen, sheriffs and members of the Common Council of London. By the time the head of the column reached St Paul's, its tail had still not left Whitehall. The route was packed with crowds, who behaved with deep, solemn reverence. The only sound to be heard resembled the quiet murmuring sea as men respectfully removed their hats.

The ceremony in the cathedral was attended by 32 admirals and more than a hundred captains. It lasted from just after 1 p.m. until about 6 p.m. The solemnity was enhanced by the necessity, as evening approached, of lighting the cathedral with candles; beneath the great dome a chandelier of 130 lamps created a brilliant focus. The coffin was lowered into the crypt beneath the dome, to be housed in the sarcophagus once intended for Cardinal Wolsey. Only the seamen's impulsive tearing of portions from the ensign of the *Victory* for themselves broke the order of proceedings.

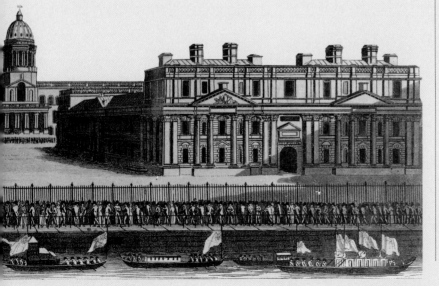

CHRONOLOGY

1758 Horatio Nelson born at Burnham Thorpe, Norfolk

1767 Catherine Nelson, his mother, dies

1771 Joins the *Raisonnable* as midshipman; transfers to the *Triumph*; sails for the West Indies in merchant vessel

1772 Rejoins the *Triumph*

1773 Joins the *Carcass* for expedition to the Arctic; joins the *Seahorse*, destined for the East Indies

1775 Opening hostilities in War of American Independence

1776 Returns home from the East Indies

1777 Passes examination for lieutenant; appointed to the *Lowestoffe*; arrives in the West Indies

1778 France allies with the American colonists against Britain; appointed first lieutenant in the *Bristol*; appointed commander of the *Badger*

1779 Appointed to the *Hinchinbrooke*; Spain allies with France against Britain

1780 Commands naval force on San Juan expedition against the Spanish; arrives in Portsmouth as an invalid

1781 Takes command of the *Albemarle*

1782 Crosses the Atlantic to Quebec; from New York proceeds to West Indies

1783 Fails to take Turks Island from the French; War of American Independence ends; stays at St Omer in France

1784 Appointed to command the *Boreas* in the West Indies; arrives at Antigua; meets Mary Moutray

1785 Meets Frances Nisbet at Nevis

1787 Marries Frances Nisbet at Nevis; returns to England; placed on half pay after *Boreas* is paid off

1788 Settles at Burnham Thorpe

1793 War against Revolutionary France begins; appointed to command the *Agamemnon*; sails for the Mediterranean with Hood's fleet; meets Hamiltons

1794 Right eye damaged at siege of Calvi, Corsica

1795 Fleet skirmish with the French; *Ça Ira* taken

1796 Promoted to commodore; transfers to the *Captain*; Spain allies with France against Britain

1797 Battle of Cape St Vincent against the Spanish; promoted rear-admiral; transfers to the *Theseus*; boat action against the Spanish off Cadiz; attack on Santa Cruz, Tenerife; loses his right arm; returns to England to recuperate

1798 Hoists flag in the *Vanguard* for the Mediterranean; Battle of the Nile against the French; returns to Naples; created Baron Nelson; evacuates Neapolitan Royal Family and Hamiltons to Palermo, Sicily

1799 Created Duke of Brontë

1800 Returns to England with the Hamiltons

1801 Promoted vice-admiral; hoists flag in the *San Josef*, then in the *St George*; Horatia born to Emma Hamilton; Battle of Copenhagen against the Danes; created Viscount Nelson; appointed to a squadron defending the English Channel; unsuccessful attack on Boulogne; buys Merton Place

1802 End of French Revolutionary War

1803 Sir William Hamilton dies; war against Napoleonic France begins; appointed Commander-in-Chief in the Mediterranean; in the *Victory* joins British fleet off Toulon

1804 Spain allies with France against Britain

1805 Pursues the French to the West Indies; stays at Merton for three weeks; rejoins British fleet off Cadiz; Battle of Trafalgar against the French; Nelson is killed

1806 State funeral in St Paul's Cathedral

NAVAL TERMS

Bomb vessel Small naval vessel strengthened to carry mortars for the bombardment of fortresses on shore.

Brig Small manoeuvrable two-masted ship carrying about 14 guns, with square sails set on both masts.

Cutter Small, fast-sailing one-masted vessel, usually armed.

First rate Largest class of warship, with 100 guns or more on three decks.

Flagship Ship carrying the officer commanding a squadron or fleet, and flying his flag, usually that of vice- or rear-admiral.

Forecastle Short deck built over the fore part of the main deck.

Foretop Top section of the foremast.

Frigate A single decked warship carrying between 24 and 44 guns.

Impressment Forced recruitment into the Royal Navy of seamen or those who worked on rivers.

Letter of marque Commission granted by the Lords Commissioners of the Admiralty to commanders of merchant ships or privateers to attack and take the vessels of an enemy power.

Line of battle Arrangement of warships in a line broadside on to an enemy with whom they intended to do battle.

Midshipman Junior officer, usually young, appointed by the captain of a warship to assist the lieutenants to manage a ship.

Orlop deck Lowest deck in a large ship, below the waterline, where the cockpit was situated and the cables were coiled.

Petty officer Experienced man, appointed by the commanding officer; some assisted warrant officers as their 'mates'.

Post-captain Captain who had received an Admiralty commission to hold that post in a specified ship.

Prize Vessel captured from an enemy or her allies.

Prize-agent Person employed to have a captured enemy vessel adjudged a lawful prize, to have it valued and sold.

Prize-money Money derived from the sale of a captured ship and divided unequally between the capturing officers and crew.

Quarter-deck Deck above the main deck running from the stern to about half-way along the length of a ship.

Schooner Fast-sailing two-masted vessel carrying sails that were set along its length, in the same plane as the keel.

Ship of the line Warship of at least 64 guns that could take its place in a line of battle; the most common type was the 74.

Warrant officer Officer employed under the authority of a warrant from the Navy Board: for example, the master, boatswain, gunner, carpenter.

Watch The period of time, normally 4 hours, or that half of the crew on look-out duty; crews were divided into port and starboard watches.

Yard Spar suspended from a mast in the horizontal position so that a square sail might be hung from it across the breadth of a ship.

IN THE FOOTSTEPS OF NELSON

NELSON WAS BORN in Burnham Thorpe, Norfolk, and lived there until going to sea with his uncle at the age of 12. He retired to Burnham Thorpe on half-pay with his bride Frances in 1788, remaining unemployed until 1793. The old parsonage was demolished in 1803 but the church of All Saints and The Plough Inn, since renamed The Lord Nelson, remain from his time.

Merton Place, at Merton in Surrey, which he bought in 1801, was demolished in 1846. But the church of St Mary the Virgin preserves the bench from the box pew in which Nelson and the Hamiltons sat. At Southside House, Wimbledon (tel. 0181 946 7643), not far away, where they enjoyed the company of the owner John Pennington, is the card table they used and the dais where Emma performed her 'Attitudes'.

Nelson first went to sea from Chatham in Kent. There the Georgian dockyard, where the *Victory* was built, has been preserved and is open to the public (tel. 01634 812551). A part of the historic dockyard at Portsmouth, in Hampshire, is also open, and there, in dry-dock off the basin, the *Victory* can be visited (tel. 01705 839755). The spot where Nelson fell is marked on her quarter-deck, as is the place in the orlop deck where he died. Nelson's cabin contains much of his original furniture, including his cot. Nearby, some of the eighteenth-century storehouses have been used to house the Royal Naval Museum (tel. 01705 875806), the contents of which include an important Nelson collection. There is his sea chest and a preparatory sketch by John Hoppner, for a finished picture now in the Royal Collection.

The greatest number of Nelson's and Emma's possessions, with the best-known portraits, are in the National Maritime Museum at Greenwich, in London (tel. 0181 858 4422). In 1995 the Museum opened a new Nelson gallery which reveals much about Nelson's legacy to the British nation. Here is displayed the bullet-holed coat and blood-stained stockings, with the breeches that had to be cut from Nelson's legs; also the jewellery that once belonged to Emma. Monmouth, in Gwent, has a Nelson Museum too (tel. 01600 713519), where the collection contains much silverware, both his own and a selection of commemorative items.

Across the road from the National Maritime Museum is the Royal Naval College, formerly the Royal Hospital for Seamen. Here, in the Painted Hall, Nelson lay in state when his body was brought back to England and before it was taken up the River Thames to London. Redolent of the debt owed to Nelson by the British nation is his tomb in the crypt of St Paul's Cathedral. Directly beneath the cathedral dome, his body lies within the Renaissance sarcophagus originally intended for Cardinal Wolsey.

Outside England, visits can be made in Corsica to the beach at Miamo, where Nelson landed guns three miles to the north of Bastia, and the gulley, Porto Agro, where he landed them for the bombardment of Calvi. In Naples, the Palazzo Reale still exists, as does Sir William's embassy, the Palazzo Sessa. Villa Emma, the Hamiltons' seaside house, also stands, above the beach at Posilippo. Nelson's own house in Sicily, Castello di Maniace, which he received with the dukedom of Brontë but never visited, is on the lower, western slopes of Mount Etna.

In Jamaica, the Fort Charles battery, which Nelson commanded in 1779, is open to visitors, as the Port Royal Museum. *El Castillo de la Immaculada Concepción,* on the San Juan river in Nicaragua, is accessible to only the most adventurous.

INDEX

ACKNOWLEDGEMENTS

The illustrations are reproduced by kind permission of the following:

Bridgeman Art Library: 26, 38, 56 (left), 114 (Fitzwilliam Museum, Cambridge); British Library: 27, 43, 48, 49, 97, 112, 134; Christie's Images: 54 (right), 96 (top), 97 (left), 115 (left), 140; Courtauld Institute of Art, Witt Library: 32; ET Archive: 2 (National Maritime Museum), 7, 11, 75, 87 (left), 102, 151 (Tate Gallery); Giraudon: 60/61, 83, 95; Lloyd's of London: 62 (left), 80, 144, 146 (left), 152 (left); Mansell Collection: 16 (top), 60 (left); Mary Evans Picture Library: 33 (bottom); National Maritime Museum, Greenwich: Front cover (both), 2, 6, 10 (both), 12, 13, 14 (both), 15, 18 (both), 19, 21 (top), 22 (right), 23, 24, 25, 29, 30, 31, 33 (top), 36 (both), 41, 42, 45, 46 (left), 47 (right), 52, 54 (left), 55, 56 (right), 59, 61, 62/63, 63, 66, 67, 69, 72, 73, 74, 76 (right), 77, 79, 84, 85, 87 (right and bottom), 94 (both), 98 (both), 100, 103, 107 (all), 111, 113, 116, 117, 119 (both), 120, 122 (right), 123, 124 (both), 126, 127, 129, 131, 132 (top), 135, 137 (right), 138, 139, 141, 142, 143, 146 (right), 147; National Portrait Gallery, London: 16 (bottom), 71, 115 (right), back cover; National Trust, Anglesey Abbey: 91; Nelson Museum, Monmouth: 17, 28 (left), 118; Private Collection (photo courtesy Agnew & Co.): 128; Clive Richards Esq: 51; The Royal Collection © Her Majesty The Queen: 39;

Royal Naval Museum, Portsmouth: 90, 122 (left); Scala (Museo Nazionale, Naples): 99; Sotheby's Transparency Library: 86; Warwick Leadlay Gallery, Greenwich: 8, 9, 50/51, 76 (left), 81, 82, 89, 92, 106 (both), 136/137, 145 (both), 149; Weidenfeld Archive: 96 (right); Yale Center for British Art, New Haven, Paul Mellon Collection: 40.

These illustrations come from the following books:
J. A. Atkinson *The Costume of Britain* (1807): 34, 35; William Hamilton *Supplement to Campi Phlegraei* (1779): 71; Frederic Hervey *Naval History of Great Britain* (1779): 21 (left), 68; J. Johnson *Views of the West Indies* (1827): 46/47; John Knox Laughton *Nelson and his Companions In Arms* (1896): 64, 78, 88; Darcy Lever *Young Officer's Sheet Anchor* (1808): 53, 132 (right); Edward Orme *Graphic History of The Life of Nelson* (1806): 3, 22 (right), 153; J. Robertson *Elements of Navigation* (1796): 1, 20, 28 (right); D. and J. T. Serres *Liber Nauticus* (1805): 44 (both), 58, 64 (right).

The publishers would like to thank Dr Pieter van der Merwe of the National Maritime Museum and Anthony Cross of Warwick Leadlay for their help.

SELECT BIBLIOGRAPHY

Clarke, James Stanier, and M'Arthur, John, *The Life of Admiral Lord Nelson K.B. from his Lordship's Manuscripts* (2 vols, London, 1809).

Gérin, Winfred, *Horatia Nelson* (London, 1970).

Harrison, James, *The Life of the Right Honourable Horatio, Lord Viscount Nelson* (2 vols, London, 1806).

Hibbert, Christopher, *Nelson. A Personal History* (London, 1994).

Laughton, Sir John Knox, *Letters and Dispatches of Horatio, Viscount Nelson* (London, 1886).

Lavery, Brian, *Nelson's Navy: The Ships, Men and Organisation 1793-1815* (London, 1989).

Layard, G. S., ed., *The Letters of Lord Nelson to Lady Hamilton with a Supplement* (2 vols, London, 1814).

Minto, Countess of, ed., *The Life and Letters of Sir Gilbert Elliot, First Earl of Minto from 1751 to 1806* (3 vols, London, 1874).

Morrison, Alfred, ed., *The Collection of Autograph Letters and Personal Documents Formed by Alfred Morrison: The Hamilton and Nelson Papers* (2 vols, 1893-4).

Naish, G. P. B., ed., *Nelson's Letters to His Wife and Other Documents, 1785-1831* (London, 1958).

Nicolas, Sir Harris, ed., *Dispatches and Letters of Vice-Admiral Lord Viscount Nelson* (7 vols, London, 1844-6).

Pocock, Tom, *Horatio Nelson* (London, 1987).

Sladen, Douglas, *Lord Nelson's Letters to Lady Hamilton* (London, 1905).